Prayer in a Troubled World

Prayer in a Troubled World

GEORGE APPLETON

Darton, Longman and Todd
London

First published 1988 by
Darton, Longman and Todd Ltd
89 Lillie Road, London SW6 1UD

© 1988 George Appleton

ISBN 0 232 51726 6

Author's royalties on this book will be used for
helping ecumenical work to provide pure drinking
water for the 75 per cent of the world's humans who
do not yet have it.

British Library Cataloguing in Publication Data

Appleton, George, *1902–*
    Prayer in a troubled world.
    1. Christian life. Prayer
    I. Title
    248.3'2

    ISBN 0–232–51726–6

Phototypeset by
Input Typesetting Ltd, London SW19 8DR
Printed and bound in Great Britain by
Anchor Brendon Ltd, Tiptree, Essex

Contents

Preface

The title of this small book has a number of deep and wide implications. It assumes a knowledge of what is going on in the world, not possible for earlier generations. Radio gives us reports of happenings a few minutes after they have taken place. Voices of people on the spot can be heard by satellite projection. Newspapers have their reporters who rush to the scene to gather exclusive stories. TV enables us to see how other people live and the disastrous consequences of many of the happenings, arousing feelings of dismay and often of compassion. The many charitable societies have fund-raisers in their employ, who are quick to bombard us with urgent appeals. We are appalled by the tragedies and crimes, and the accompanying devaluation of human life. In it all we are becoming world citizens, slowly realising we have a responsibility for the whole human family.

Those of us who believe that there is a spiritual constituent in the make-up of human personality, feel that the problem facing us is a spiritual one, which urges us to pray, and so keep God from being forgotten or pushed out. Far too often we tell God what we think he ought to do, which amounts to praying for the success of our own ideas rather than his.

Much depends on what kind of God we believe him to be, a loving and saving God, whose wisdom, love and goodness are available to all if we put ourselves in his hands to produce the kind of world he wants and the happiness of every human being in every generation.

More than this, he is willing to come and live in the core or heart of every human being, to guard us from evil and to guide us into right living and loving. Those of us who believe that he exists are fortunate in having a picture of what he is, and what he wills, in human terms in the life, death and survival of Jesus Christ. We are learning that God is completely free to tackle any situation; he will not be bound by any man-made rules, systems or methods.

We are learning how to pray in this entirely new situation. It is in silence that we experience his nearness and newness. Jesus has taught us that true prayer does not consist in our speaking much. We must listen as well as speak, and the more we find ourselves unable to put our thoughts, feelings and desires into words, the more hope there is of hearing the silent words he puts into our hearts.

In the pattern prayer Jesus gave us, he taught us to pray for God to rule in our hearts and affairs, and to long for his wise, loving will to be done, not in sad resignation, but in joyful trust and longing. It is my hope and prayer that this book may help myself and others to love him with all our being, and to love others as brothers and sisters in his all-inclusive family.

†GEORGE APPLETON
Lent 1988

Acknowledgements

Thanks are due to the following for permission to quote copyright material:

Juliet Boobbyer and Joanna Sciortino, from *Columba* published by Fowler Wright Books Ltd; Central Board of Finance of the Church of England, from *Faith in the City* (Church House Publishing, 1985); Collins Fount, from *Journey for a Soul* by George Appleton, *The Coming of God* by Maria Boulding, *The Gospels in Modern English* by J. B. Phillips in *The New Testament in Modern English*, and the daily prayer of Mother Teresa of Calcutta quoted in *Something Beautiful for God* by Malcolm Muggeridge; The Executors of the Estate of C. Day Lewis, 'A Carol' from *Collected Poems 1954* published by the Hogarth Press and from 'Offertorium' from *Requiem of the Living* in *The Gate* published by Jonathan Cape Ltd; Eyre & Spottiswoode Publishers, Her Majesty's Printers, London, extracts from the Book of Common Prayer 1662, the rights of which are vested in the Crown within the United Kingdom; Hodder & Stoughton Ltd, prayers by Frank Coloquhoun, Christopher Idle and Dick Williams from *New Parish Prayers* edited by Frank Coloquhoun; Lutterworth Press, from *In His Name* by George Appleton; A. R. Mowbray & Co Ltd, from *The Prayer Manual* by F. N. MacNutt; John Murray (Publishers) Ltd, from *A Chain of Prayer Across the Ages* by Selina Fox; the National Society (Church of England) for Promoting Religious Education, from *Hymns and Songs for Children* edited by Margaret Cropper; SLG Press, from the article by Mother Jane in *Fairacres Chronicle* (Winter 1987); SPCK, from *Glad Encounter, Jerusalem Prayers, One Man's Prayers* and *The Word is the Seed* by George Appleton; the Revd Victor Stock, 'A prayer for one who took her own life' quoted in *Fairacres Chronicle* (Spring 1987); World Council of Churches, from *WCC Bulletin* (Vancouver Assembly 1983).

Every effort has been made to identify and acknowledge quotations; but both author and publisher are aware that there remain a few omissions and would welcome information which would enable them to correct these in future editions of this book.

1

Introduction

No one who studies the news every day can doubt that we live in a very troubled world. A spiritual teacher from the East, the Dalai Lama, who in exile from his own land of Tibet and in his worldwide travels has become one of the greatest teachers and prophets of our present age, revered by millions, sums it up for us:

> When we rise in the morning and listen to the radio or read the newspaper, we are confronted with the same sad news: violence, crime, wars and disasters. I cannot recall a single day without a report of something terrible somewhere. Even in these modern times it is clear that one's precious life is not safe. No former generation has had to experience so much bad news as we face today; this constant awareness of fear and tension should make any sensitive and compassionate person question seriously the progress of our modern world.

Like all enlightened Buddhist followers in every generation, the Dalai Lama is sensitively aware of the universal phenomenon of evil and suffering. His vocation is to show people everywhere the way of liberation, happiness and peace.

Nearly seventy years ago at the Peace Conference which followed the First World War, General Smuts foresaw the great changes ahead and warned the national leaders of their approach.

Mankind is once more on the move. The very foundations have been shaken and loosened, and things are again fluid. The tents have been struck, and the great caravan of humanity is once more on the march. Vast social and industrial changes are coming, perhaps upheavals which may, in their magnitude and effects, be comparable to war itself.

2,500 years ago one of the great Hebrew prophets, the second Isaiah, looking at the return of Jewish exiles from Babylon, heard within his heart what he believed was a message from the God they worshipped: 'Look, the former things have come to pass, and new things I now declare unto you, before they spring forth I tell you of them' (Isa. 42:9).

John, who understood Jesus more deeply than any other of his fellow-disciples, in exile in old age on the island of Patmos, heard the crucified, risen and glorified Christ say to him: 'Look, I am making all things new' (Rev. 21:5).

The poet Tennyson, aware of great changes taking place in the late nineteenth century, and also aware that long-established customs tend to lose their dynamic and inspirational qualities, wrote:

> The old order changeth, yielding place to new
> And God reveals Himself in many ways,
> Lest one good custom should corrupt the world.

Those of us who believe in God as Creator of all also believe that he is always active among those he has created, active in many different ways according to their experience of him, their own history and culture. Many people in a period of unrest, widespread breakdown and suffering ask, 'Whatever is God doing?' as if he were responsible for all that happens. Those who have come to know something of him through teachers and prophets, and even more through saintly souls, and still more through prayer, meditation and consciousness of his presence always and everywhere, believe he is bringing a new order to birth, because the old order is no longer advancing his eternal purpose of love. So he bids us search for him at work, and as we begin to discover him, to co-operate with him in creating the world of his will.

The writers of the New Testament believed that in Christ the eternal God was revealing his being, nature and will. They do not underestimate the fallen nature and sins of us humans, but emphasise the initiative of God in Christ in reconciling the world to himself. Paul takes up this theme of something new taking the place of what is old:

> From now on, therefore, we regard no one from a human point of view; even though we once regarded Christ from a human point of view, we regard him thus no longer. Therefore, if any one is in Christ, he is a new creation; the old has passed away, behold, the new has come. All this is from God, who through Christ reconciled us to himself and gave us the ministry of reconciliation; that is, in Christ God was reconciling the world to himself, not counting their trespasses against them, and entrusting to us the message of reconciliation. So we are ambassadors for Christ, God making his appeal through us. We beseech you on behalf of Christ, be reconciled to God. (2 Cor. 5:16–20)

Individual believers as well as the body of Christian believers must bear part of the responsibility for the condition of the world. If we were only more holy and loving, growing more like the Master whose disciples we claim to be, and the God whom he revealed in his perfection of love and unlimited forgiveness, the world would be a better place.

John, spoken of as 'the disciple whom Jesus loved' and equally the disciple who loved Jesus, crystallised the good news of his birth, life, death and survival which we speak of as the resurrection, and reception into God which we call the ascension, all summarised in very simple clear words which anyone can understand: GOD SO LOVED THE WORLD. He will go on loving the world, forgiving its sins, healing its tragedies until the end of time and beyond. It may take millions of years, much aching of the divine heart, many tears over the foolishnesses, tragedies and crimes of us humans, but his mercy and love endure for ever. God still loves the world. Blessed be God.

2

Humanity Coming of Age

One of the insights or claims of our modern era is that man has come of age and has accepted responsibility for himself and his environment. He is no longer at the mercy of circumstances. Rivers can be diverted or dammed, mountains can be levelled, deserts irrigated, epidemics prevented. He can circle the earth and land on the planets. He is tempted to think that he is all-sufficient, that he has no need to depend on higher powers. He hopes to postpone death and thinks he can do without God.

Any parent has seen this happening in the coming of age of adolescent children, accompanied by tensing frustrations, the desire to be oneself, the choice of a profession, the search for a congenial job in a time of high unemployment, impatience with delays and obstacles, the desire to be like others in the same age group, dislike of discipline or controlling authority, complicated by the awakening of the sexual instinct. This is a difficult age for the growing adolescent to understand and undergo, hard also for parents and elders, who tend to forget that they were once in the same situation or are anxious lest their children should make the same mistakes which they actually or nearly made.

What is true of the individual now needs to be seen to be happening to humanity as a whole in ethnic, social, economic and political groups. We talk of a generation gap, and the need of community, learning to live together, accepting growing pains by those still growing, the equally willing acceptance by older people of declining powers and not resenting having to retire or 'being put on the shelf'.

Dr Charles Raven, a good friend of mine, formerly Master of Christ's College, Cambridge and Regius Professor of Divinity, used to emphasise that what we have learnt about growth in personal maturity now has to be learnt and lived in community:

We owe a great debt to Freud and his colleagues for revealing to us that from the moment of conception each one of us enters into a world of personal relationships; for developing methods for our release from the fixations and complexes of our infancy; and for enabling us to 'know ourselves, accept ourselves and be ourselves'. But psychologists, like physicians, have been content to tend the solitary individual and to adjust him to an acceptance of his environment – that is, to bring him to a state of healthy adolescence, and leave him there. They have not striven to study the nature of community and the conditions of social health or to fit their patients for the maturity in which the individual finds his fulfilment in corporate life, in the service of his fellows and the control of his environment.

Dr Raven adds his own clarifying convictions:

We cannot live without community and have begun to discover that we cannot live with it; for it has not yet been created in our urbanized and industrial areas, and is now almost lost even in the villages of the countryside. If the pioneers of mental health will show us what are the essential conditions for a true corporate life, and how the individual can free himself from the mass-behaviour of the crowd or the *führer-prinzip* of the group and find his true freedom in its creative and organic energy, we may discover the neighbourliness for which the whole world waits and the universal fellowship in which the age-old barriers of race and class and sex no longer prove insurmountable.

Every disciple of Jesus realises the importance of personal conversion and a new life not just as a single event but as an on-going deepening process. This implies a consequent membership in the kingdom of God in creating the community which will embody the vision of worldwide responsibility and neighbourly care.

The following prayers express this vision:

O God, who hast bound us together in this bundle of life, give us grace to understand how our lives depend upon the courage, the industry, the honesty, and the integrity of our fellow men; that we may be mindful of their needs, grateful for their faithfulness, and faithful in our responsibilities to them; through Jesus Christ our Lord.

Reinhold Niebuhr

A radiation prayer
May the peace which passes understanding
possess the minds of men everywhere,
banishing all anxiety and perplexity,
watching sentinel over their hearts and minds,
refusing entrance to every disturbing thought.
In everything that happens
may men know that all things work together for good
when they love thee and want thy will.
Give them thine own peace,
which the world cannot give and cannot take away.
Let nations live together in peace
and know the things that belong unto peace.
And may thy peace in my heart
go out to all my fellow men –
to clam their worries and their enmities,

to let them know that the peace given me
is available for them also,
through him who made himself men's Peace,
even Jesus Christ, our Lord.

G.A.

Lord of the nations, Creator, Redeemer and Father of all men, we thank Thee for the vision of thy purpose to gather all nations into a commonwealth of justice, peace and brotherhood. We thank thee for the United Nations Organization with its aim to avoid war, with its service in production of food, its promotion or education and health, its care of refugees and children. Guide all the nations and their leaders, we pray Thee, into deeper unity, greater efforts for peace, more generous contributions to human welfare, that men may live free from fear and free from want, and help Thee to build the universe of thy love.

G.A.

3

Testing the Foundations

Often in the history of God's people, believers in him have felt that they were living in periods of crisis and violent change, when things seemed not only to be out of their hands, but out of God's hands as well. At such times they spoke of the very foundations of the earth and human society being shaken. One of the psalmists lamented that people 'will not be learned nor understand, but walk on still in darkness: all the foundations of the earth are out of course' (Ps. 82:5). Another had a deeper faith: 'He (God) laid the foundations of the earth, that it never should move at any time' (Ps. 104:5). A further writer, worried at the sufferings of the innocent, hears God speaking within him in reproach, 'Where were you when I laid the foundations of the earth? Tell me if you have understanding', and goes on to the mysteries of the natural world (Job 38:4; 39), implying that there are mysteries in the spiritual and moral world as well.

One of the writers of the New Testament, listing the heroes of faith in the past, speaks of Abraham's faith 'that he looked forward to a city which has foundations, whose builder and maker is God' (Heb. 11:10). The same writer later adds, 'Yet once more I will shake not only the earth but heaven.' This phrase 'yet once more' indicates the removal of what is shaken, as of what has been made, in order that 'what cannot be shaken may remain'. He concludes: 'Therefore . . . let us be grateful for receiving a kingdom that cannot be shaken' (12:26–28).

9

It is easier for the human mind to be aware of the shakable things than of the things that cannot be shaken. We see old houses falling into decay and great buildings demolished in a second by bombs planted within them or by missiles fired from a distance, and people searching for things they treasured or frantically digging for trapped relatives whose cries or tapping can attract attention for a desperately short time.

What are the unshakable things that will never wear out and will never disappear? The apostle Paul who had undergone almost every conceivable hardship and been involved in many dangerous situations – shipwreck, imprisonment, scourgings, hunger, thirst, plots and false accusations, anxiety for his converts (reading his own catalogue in 2 Cor. 11:24–28) – said that there were three indestructible things: faith, hope and love. To him faith was trust in God whatever happened. All his hope was founded on God, seeing God's purpose for the whole human race which enabled him to continue undaunted in well-nigh hopeless circumstances. The third indestructible was love which he regarded as the greatest of the three, God's eternal love for every individual and for the whole world.

The apostle John says in very clear and simple words that love is the most characteristic feature of God, in fact he identifies God with love and asserts 'We know we have passed out of death into life because we love the brethren. He who does not love remains in death' (1 John 3:14; 4:7–12).

Every man, in the course of his life, must not only show himself obedient and docile. By his fidelity he must build – starting with the most natural territory of his own self – a work . . . into which something enters from all the elements of the earth. He makes his own soul throughout all his earthly days; and at the same time he collaborates in another work, which infinitely transcends . . . the perspectives of his individual achievement: the completing of the world.

Teilhard de Chardin

O almighty God, who hast built thy Church upon the foundation of the apostles and prophets, Jesus Christ himself being the head corner-stone: Grant us so to be joined together in unity of spirit by their doctrine, that we may be made an holy temple acceptable unto thee; through Jesus Christ our Lord.

Collect for St Simon and St Jude's day
BCP (1928)

4

Becoming World Citizens

St Paul was an educated Roman citizen, proud of the city
of Tarsus where he grew up; he studied under a famous
rabbi in Jerusalem, and after his conversion to Christ spent
some years in Arabia, called by his friend Barnabas, a
Cypriot, to take part in the active Christian community in
Antioch, with its outward look and world view. It was there
that he and Barnabas were commissioned to go out on a
first missionary journey to Cyprus and Galatia to spread the
good news of what God had done in Jesus, whom he now
accepted as the Messiah or Christ, not only of Jews but of
Gentiles also. He now saw that his own vocation was to
'bring salvation to the uttermost parts of the earth' (Acts
13:47).

On a second journey Paul crossed over into Europe,
landing at Philippi, a significant extension of his vision and
mission. From there he went on to Salonika and Athens
where he spoke to a crowd of learned people – philosophers
and seekers for anything new. His starting point was an altar
with the inscription 'To God unknown' and the claim that
God had made himself known to people of every nation as
one in whom we live and move and have our being, who is
not remote from any, but will judge the world in righteousness by one whom he has appointed and for whom he has
stood guarantee by raising him from the dead.

From Athens Paul went on to Corinth, a busy cosmo-
politan seaport where he stayed over a year, earning his own

living and building up a strong Christian community to which
he later wrote at least two long pastoral letters.

Learning that there was a severe famine in the province
of Syria, Paul organised a collection for the poor Christians
in Jerusalem which he took there on a quick visit, evidence
of the growth of a widening community.

His ambition was to visit Rome, the capital of the empire,
and after that Spain. Ultimately he did arrive at Rome, but
as a prisoner (Acts 28:14–31). From prison he wrote at least
three pastoral letters – Ephesians, Philippians and Colossians
– and a personal letter to Philemon sending back to him a
runaway slave, who had been converted as a result of his
contact with Paul in prison. In these three letters he works
out his conviction about the world significance of Jesus. In
Ephesians he writes: 'God has made known to us in all
wisdom and insight the mystery (*secret*) of his will, according
to his purpose which he set forth in Christ as a plan for the
fulness of time, to unite all things in heaven and things on
earth' (1:9–10). In a later chapter he becomes more explicit,
claiming that Gentiles are fellow-heirs, members of the same
body and partakers of the promise in Christ Jesus through
the gospel (3:6).

In Colossians he makes the same point: 'Here there cannot
be Greek and Jew, circumcised and uncircumcised,
barbarian, Scythian, slave, free man, but Christ is all in
all' (3:11). Christian discipleship rises above all differences,
religious, racial, cultural, economic. In Galatians 3:28 Paul
adds, 'neither male nor female', implying that in Christ
difference even of sex is transcended.

The writer of the fourth gospel puts this in another way
when he speaks of the high priest Caiaphas wanting to liqui-
date Jesus: 'It is expedient that one should die for the people,
and that the whole nation should not perish.' The evangelist
interprets this, 'and not for the nation only, but to gather
into one the children of God who are scattered abroad'. To
John, Christ is the Gatherer, gathering into one all truth and

all people. The whole of humanity is to be gathered into the community of God.

So to those of us who call ourselves Christians there are three kinds of citizenship: citizens of our native country; citizens of the world, the international community; and the governing citizenship of the kingdom of heaven (Phil. 3:20). Of this third citizenship Sir Cecil Spring Rice, Ambassador to the USA during the First World War, on the night before he died, wrote:

> And there's another country, I've heard of long ago,
> Most dear to them that love her, most great to them
>   that know;
> We may not count her armies, we may not see her king;
> Her fortress is a faithful heart, her pride is suffering;
> And soul by soul and silently, her shining bounds
>   increase,
> And her ways are ways of gentleness and all her paths
>   of peace.

Songs of Praise 319

A superficial study of the war years and the post-war years might suggest that there has been a failure or even refusal to move forward towards the goal of international relationship. So many new nations have come into being and have copied the rival and competitive pattern of the colonial powers from whom they have gained independence. It is true that the British Empire of imperial power has become a commonwealth of free association, with a wider membership than the largely white self-governing dominions. The United Nations Organisation has over 150 member nations, with non-voting rights for non-governmental organisations, who in the lobbies of the great headquarters can exert influence and even pressure, but progress is still slow in the acceptance of an international outlook.

On the other hand it is true that until people have experienced nationhood they cannot be expected to move forward to inter-nationhood. It may be that the recognition and practice of interdependence will in time bring this about. The recent mandate for the cessation of the war between Iran and Iraq and the aim that the shipping of all nations shall be protected could be another birth pang in the coming of a new order.

A small olive branch may be seen in the extra verses to the national anthem of Great Britain which were composed over a century ago by the hymn writer W. E. Hickson (1803–70), of which the last verse was the most prophetic:

> Not on this land alone –
> But be God's mercies known
>   From shore to shore.
> Lord, make the nations see
> That men should brothers be,
> And form one family
>   The wide world o'er.

5

Warning Prophets

Many of us would like to know the future, our personal future, and that of the world. Astrologers profess to know what the stars tell us, palmists study the markings on our hands and predict what is about to happen to us. Many newspapers and magazines have their weekly forecasts which millions read. Opinion polls take a sample of the public and deduce what will be the result of elections if people do not change their minds before polling day, admitting that there may still be a considerable percentage who have not yet made a decision or decline to say. Bookmakers draw up tables of betting odds as to horses' chances in a race, or of the candidates for an important appointment, even bishoprics. Tipsters offer their nap selections, either free or for payment for supposedly inside information.

Cranks pretend to know the date of the end of the world. When I was in Jerusalem I received a letter ordering me to summon the heads of the Middle East nations to assemble at the Mount of Olives at 4 a.m. on a certain Sunday. I realised that 4 a.m. was a little too early for most of the national leaders as well as myself, and the day came and went without the prophesied happening. I was disturbed to learn afterwards that one of my clergy friends did attend, and had been disappointed with the poor attendance and finally returned to his home tired and hungry, for breakfast.

Some readers of the Bible think the prophets foretold what was certain to happen. They were more like the opinion

16

polls so common today. They always included in their message the significant hope 'if things don't change', and they hoped and pleaded that people would change, so that the disastrous consequences need not happen. In many cases people did not change, and the inevitable results took place, and people blamed God.

'If things don't change' is the warning of the prophets. 'Things must change' has an implicit hope about it, and the earlier that message gets across and is put into practice the more confident the hope. St Paul warned his early converts: 'Do not be deceived; God is not mocked, for whatever a man sows, that he will also reap. For he who sows to his own flesh, will from the flesh reap corruption; but he who sows to the Spirit will from the Spirit reap eternal life (Gal. 6:7–8).

Before Paul, Jesus saw how easy it was for his disciples to use pious words: 'Not every one who says to me, "Lord, Lord" shall enter the kingdom of heaven, but he who does the will of my Father who is in heaven' (Matt. 7:21). He does not expect us to do this unaided, for God gives his help, will guide us with his wisdom, and even comes to live in the depths of our personality that we speak of as our 'heart' or 'spirit'. Unlimited grace is available for us, and unlimited forgiveness, not only for actual sins, but also for our failure to come near to his holiness and love (Rom. 3:23).

We do not know what the immediate future holds. From the teaching of Jesus, from our own experience of God in prayer and meditation, from the evidence of St Paul and St John, we can be sure of God's love for the world and every created being: 'God so loves the world . . . God sent not his Son into the world to condemn the world, but that the world through him might be saved . . . it is not the will of my Father who is in heaven that one of these little ones perish . . . God our Saviour desires all to be saved and come to the knowledge of the truth.'

And 'No eye has seen, nor ear heard, nor the heart of man conceived, what God has prepared for those who love him' (1 Cor. 2:9). I dare to add to this further insight from St Paul 'and for those who do not yet do so', hoping that this is in keeping, one of the revealings of Julian, the saintly hermitress of Norwich who lived as recently, or as long ago, as the thirteenth century: 'All shall be well, all manner of things shall be well.' That is the will of God and we can be sure that he will be working to accomplish it not only in this world but in the world after death.

The following prayers have helped me:

O God, who hast prepared for them that love thee (*and for those who do not yet do so*) such good things as pass man's understanding; pour into our hearts such love toward thee, that we, loving thee above all things, may obtain thy promises, which exceed all that we can desire; through Jesus Christ our Lord.

BCP, Trinity VI

Withhold not from me, O my God, the best, the Spirit of thy dear Son; that in that day when the judgment is set I may be presented unto Thee not blameless, but forgiven, not effectual but faithful, not holy but persevering, without desert but accepted, because he hath pleaded the causes of my soul, and redeemed my life.

Eric Milner-White

Grant, O Lord, we beseech thee, that the course of this world may be so peaceably ordered by thy governance, that (*the nations*) may joyfully serve thee in all godly quietness; through Jesus Christ our Lord.

BCP, Trinity V

6

Religions Talking Together

The great missionary conference at Edinburgh in 1910 awakened the Christian churches to their task of mission. It was attended by 1200 delegates; all except a small handful of invited guests were from the missionary churches of the West. It was followed by the formation of national missionary councils in many countries and notably by the International Missionary Council. During the twentieth century there has been a most significant increase in indigenous ministers and leaders, resulting in independent churches.

Another significant development from Edinburgh has been a first-hand contact with members of world religions other than the Christian and an awakening to their own faiths, founders and scriptures, accompanied by a changed attitude in the Christian churches towards them, no longer thinking and speaking of them as heathen and pagans. Christian belief in God as Creator and of all created in the divine image has inspired the conviction that he loves all and is in his own divine way active among them all. Belief in the spiritual nature of man has also resulted in an interest in their spiritual experience, together with a realisation of responsibility for the peace of the world and the welfare of all its peoples.

This new understanding has also been reciprocal, with people of other faiths looking at Christians in a new way, with a readiness to explain their own faith and also listen to

19

the experience and faith of others. We talk together, opening mind and heart to each other, learning that we share a common humanity. Milestones in this new development in the Christian Church have been the founding of the International Missionary Council in 1921, the World Council of Churches in 1948, and later the uniting of these two great international bodies.

The saintly Cardinal Bea was not only a great worker for Christian unity but also for a new attitude towards other faiths. At a gathering in 1962 in Rome of leaders from world religions he made this declaration:

> Perhaps few among you have so many dealings with men of different races, different religions, different beliefs and different cultures as I – unworthily – have. In all these dealings I have always found a great love, a wide-open heart, always opens the hearts of others. This great love must be not mere diplomacy but the result of a sincere conviction that, as I have already said, we are all the children of one God, who has created mankind, who has created each one of us, and whose children we all are.

A further great occasion was the meeting at Assisi in October 1986 of the leaders of the Christian churches and representatives of the other world religions, at the invitation of Pope John Paul II. On this occasion members of the different world faiths prayed simultaneously but separately for the peace of the world, following their own customs of prayer, and then met together for biddings and silent prayer. The theme of the whole meeting was 'Together in Prayer for Peace'. Among the Christian leaders present were Archbishop Robert Runcie as Head of the Anglican Communion, Cardinal Basil Hume, representing the Episcopal Conferences of Western Europe, and the General Secretary of the World Council of Churches as well as several of its Presidents. Shortly after this great day Cardinal Hume and Archbishop Runcie selected a splendidly ecumenical (in its sense of 'worldwide') collection of readings and prayers, which is now being used throughout the English-speaking world. Unnumbered pray-ers and workers for peace will want to offer their own *Te Deum laudamus* for what was initiated at Assisi in October 1986.

Among prayers which Christians may pray and others overhear and perhaps adapt to their own devotional expression are the following:

O God, I gaze in wonder at thy creative love, at thy seeking for people everywhere and their search for Thee, showing Thyself in ways they can understand. Help me to learn more of Thee from the experience of other communities of faith, and so to live and love that others may learn to share what I have found of Thee in Jesus Christ. Open my eyes, enlighten my mind, enlarge my heart, and grant that my own expression of Thee in life and word may come closer to thy eternal truth and love. O God, my God, God of all.

G.A.

O Spirit of God, guide me
As I seek to discover thy working
with men of other faiths.
Give me the strength of truth,
The gentleness and strength of love,
The clear eye of judgment, and the courage of faith.
Above all, grant me a deeper understanding
of him who is the truth,
a greater commitment to him who is the Lord,
a deeper gratitude to him
who is the Saviour of all,
even Jesus Christ thy eternal Word,
through whom thou art drawing all men
to Thyself, that they may be saved for ever,

and worship Thee the only God
blessed for evermore.

Prayer for people in their own religious settings
O Eternal Being and Reality, Origin and Goal of all
    beings and things, Lord of a hundred Names,
Let the people of each religion live by its central faith,
    glad in its own gospel.
Let us Christians be faithful to the revelation of Thee in
    Christ Jesus, sharing his mind and character . . .
Let none of us claim to have the whole truth,
Let all of us welcome the truth which others live by.

G.A.
from *Glad Encounter*

7

An Age of Protest

This is not only an age of protest but also one of pressure groups, organised marches and demonstrations. There can be a positive element in this, for politicians are as fallible as the rest of us. That is democracy – not just the thoughtless views of one section of a nation, but the consideration of what is good for all, and the motive of setting right what is a resented injustice to any section.

Sometimes protest is both right and necessary, as many feel about colour-prejudice, racial superiority and proud selfish apartheid, but for followers of Christ protest must be without ill-will and malice. It must be persuasive, almost regretful, continuing until any injustice is set right. Surely also there must be recognition of any forward step on the part of those we criticise, without ceasing to point out that there is still a long way to go before we get a society that is just to all.

One of the problems is that often people in authority take little notice of feelings of injustice until those working for reform make a nuisance of themselves, or in elections threaten marginal seats. Public opinion must always be recognised as a factor in any particular situation, even if it is thought to be wrong, in which case it needs to be changed without falling into an opposite extreme.

Another mistake lovers of the Bible sometimes make is that made by Paul when he wrote, 'The powers that be are ordained by God' (Rom. 13:1), and are not a terror to those who do right. I cannot help wishing he had added a disclaimer that this was his own opinion rather than a word from God, as he did in another context (1 Cor. 7:12).

Having said that, I must be careful not to claim that anything I think or say or write is God's infallible truth. I only hope and pray that God will give me a right judgment in all things, as the Church prays in the Book of Common Prayer collect for Pentecost (Whitsun), which goes back to Pope Gregory who sent Augustine of Canterbury to convert us not-knowing-gospel people of England.

It may be that Paul, as a Roman citizen in the provinces, admired the empire's reputation for law and justice, and wanted all fellow citizens to make a stand for those two great principles. He certainly urged people to pay taxes, something we need to think about, for governments only have what their citizens raise. Christians are expected to go further, not only to love others as much as they love themselves (equal justice for all), but to love others as Christ does, something universal and unlimited.

Paul concludes his argument with the over-arching principle of Philippians 3:20 'Our citizenship is in heaven', and in that verse we can perceive final guidance and authentic authority. He urges us to pray for our rulers, that they may accept God's righteousness and inspiration as that to which we give intention of obedience, recognising that it applies to ourselves as well as to our representatives and governments.

Prayer for a better order

Behold, O Lord God, our strivings after a truer and more abiding order. Give us visions that bring back a lost glory to the earth, and dreams that foreshadow the better order which Thou hast prepared for us. Scatter every excuse of frailty and unworthiness; consecrate us all with a heavenly mission: open to us a clearer prospect of our work. Give us strength according to our day gladly to welcome and gratefully to fulfil it; through Jesus Christ our Lord.

Bishop Westcott

Penitence for social disorder
Almighty God, who hast entrusted this earth unto the children of men, and through thy Son Jesus Christ hast called us unto a heavenly citizenship: Grant us we humbly beseech Thee such shame and repentance for the disorder and injustice and cruelty which are in the world that fleeing unto Thee for pardon and for grace, we may henceforth set ourselves to establish that city which has justice for its foundation and love for its law, whereof Thou art the Architect and Maker; through the same Lord Jesus Christ, thy Son, our Saviour.

Archbishop William Temple

Prayer for social justice and peace
O God, the King of righteousness, lead us we pray Thee in the ways of justice and of peace: inspire us to break down all tyranny and oppression, to gain for every man his due reward and from every man his due service; that each may live for all and all may care for each, in the Name of Jesus Christ.

Archbishop William Temple

all from F. B. MacNutt, *The Prayer Manual*

8

The Welfare State

A great new factor in our twentieth century is the high figure of unemployed following the two world wars, amounting to three million in 1987, and suggesting that human society cannot afford both war and prosperity. In my first curacy in Stepney in 1925–7, dockers in East London were lucky if they got two days casual work in any week. Food was consequently scarce, often children in our church schools were absent because they had no shoes to wear. There was as yet no unemployment benefit, and looking back I thank God that things have changed, even though many would prefer a higher rate of unemployment benefit rather than the reduction of income tax. At the same time it can be argued that any reduction in inflation results in the rates of social benefits retaining or even improving their original value.

It should be remembered too that many women are being employed either full or part-time and are showing equal skill and efficiency, though there is still imbalance in the number elected to parliament and public bodies.

We can all thank God for the founding of the welfare state under the leadership of Attlee and Beveridge, which has become the envy of other countries, as I discovered in my ministry overseas.

Machines can now do most of the heavy tasks in daily work, computers can do our calculations in record time and store our facts and recall them by pressing a button or two. Fewer workers are required. Unemployed people feel frustrated that they are making little or no contribution to the social welfare and are 'at a loose end'; school-leavers find few jobs available; and the children of unemployed parents want the same nice clothes and pocket money as their friends from prosperous homes.

There is a feeling that many unemployed may never again have the benefit of regular well-paid work. There is a small minority who will never want to do so, but it seems foolish to spend too much time and energy on preventing this, rather than tackling the main problem. It will need all our combined wisdom and efforts – government, employers, trade unions, workers, investors, social workers and the unemployed themselves – to rethink our way of living together and our responsibility for our neighbours.

Pastoral relationship and friendship reveal needs and possibilities. Many wish that the benefits, and they are many (if they can be explained simply), could be paid weekly rather than fortnightly, for it takes discipline to plan for the longer period, and the temptation to live well for the first day or two is understandably strong.

Winter is the critical time: '50p for the electric' is soon exhausted, and some saving in the summer months, to be drawn on when winter comes, would be wise foresight. For homeless people pubs are the warmest places to shelter in on days of cold and wet, but understandably landlords and bar attendants expect some custom, and beer is nearly a pound a pint. Many TV serials show clients with a pint in their hands, whereas in my far-off youth a half-pint was the normal.

One can go on endlessly describing the negative and short-comings of our situation. The aim of this book is to think out how to pray and then to pray. Prayer links us and our less fortunate neighbours with a God of compassion, love and practical wisdom, and to consult him is to be shown what one can do as an individual and as a member of a group, as a citizen in our own country and as a world citizen.

St Paul gives us a splendid and exaggeratedly expressed insight for faith and action: 'The foolishness of God is wiser than men, and the weakness of God is stronger than men' (1 Cor. 1:25).

There are changes that threaten the welfare state. One is the failure to realise that governments can only spend on welfare services the money they raise through taxation. Any increase in taxes is likely to be unpopular and be reflected in opinion polls and even electoral prospects. There are people in all political parties who care for the needs of poorer citizens. They could make it known to their leaders that they will get support if they decide to devote a proposed reduction of two or three pence in the pound to bettering conditions for those in need, even admitting that there will be a small percentage of the beneficiaries who will misuse or waste it.

Another danger is the overgrowth of the bureaucratic outlook and practice, which tends to forget the humanistic principles which inspired the founding of the welfare state and which should govern all who engage in its administration. A peace poem published in the bulletin of the European Youth Centre reflects another aspect somewhat cynically of the bureaucratic temptation:

> These high echoing chambers
> Hold dusty references to
> A thousand paper wars;
> It is surprising to find
> These white papers so clean,
> These revolutions so pristine,
> So unmarked by their contents . . .
> All so quietly and logically marked,
> Discussed, deplored, voted on, and
> Filed away.

Nor should we forget the pressure on those who have to

deal with unemployment payments and social benefits who are our representatives in welfare services and have to deal all day long with a succession of anxious and sometimes impatient applicants. Unfailing courtesy is a gift of grace.

O blessed Lord, who by the example of thy work at Nazareth hast sanctified our daily toil, and by thy teaching hast revealed the sympathy of God in our common task, grant that in the midst of our work we may find rest and peace in thy presence and may take joy in all that ministers to thy service, and the welfare of all your children; Who art ever our Refuge, our Strength and our exceeding great Reward.

Selina Fitzherbert Fox
from *A Chain of Prayer Across the Ages*

O God, Who hast bound us together in this bundle of life, give us grace to understand how our lives depend upon the courage, the industry, the honesty, and the integrity of our fellow-men; that we may be mindful of their needs, grateful for their faithfulness, and faithful in our responsibilities to them; through Jesus Christ our Lord.

Reinhold Niebuhr
from F. B. MacNutt, *The Prayer Manual*

O Lord, Who hast taught us that our citizenship is in heaven: prosper, we pray Thee, our efforts to fashion our citizenship here on earth after the pattern of the heavenly city, whose light is thy glory, and whose builder and maker Thou art; through Him whom Thou hast sent to deliver us from all evil, in our cities and in our souls, Jesus Christ our Lord.

F. B. MacNutt
from *The Prayer Manual*

9

Disturbing Facts

Ten years ago we were told by the Stockholm Institute of Peace Studies that the population of the world was 4000 million. It is now estimated to be around 4500 million and we are warned that by the year 2000, if the present rate of growth continues, it will be over 6000 million.

At the same time we were told that the global military spending amounted to 400,000 million dollars every year, twice as much as on health and half as much again as on education. Inflation, fortunately being reduced, still increases expenditure on all three counts. Money loses its value.

Cardinal Basil Hume has shocked us with the fact that 12 million children under five die every year from malnutrition and disease. We who live in countries which have adopted the welfare state are living longer, through getting more care from social workers and social services. That fact seems to widen the gap between undernourished countries and those whose people live in comparative comfort.

Having lived twenty-five years in tropical climates I know the need of water both for drinking and for the growing of food. Recently I was dismayed to learn that 3000 million people in the world do not get pure drinking water, and so are too weak to undertake the work necessary to produce more food. On top of this 700 million adults are unable to read and write, and 250 million children under fourteen do not attend school.

Another startling figure is that well over half the population of the world live in countries which have more than 1000 inhabitants per doctor.

The Stockholm Institute tells us that a reduction of even 5 per cent in the armaments budget could take care of the needs I have mentioned. The United Nations Organisation calculates that if every country, rich and poor, gave 0.7 of 1 per cent of its Gross National Product world poverty could be banished in a generation. Seven-tenths of 1 per cent?

The Scandinavian countries come near to this figure. The present world average is 0.37 per cent. The figure for the UK is 0.34 per cent, and the US, in spite of its massive giving and the memory of the Marshall Plan, gives a smaller percentage than the UK.

It is also estimated that 300 million people live in slums and shanty towns. Having knocked around the world a good deal I would think that figure was on the low side.

Anyone who has seen the many homeless people sleeping on the streets of Calcutta or living in cardboard shacks in parts of Cairo, or heard Mother Teresa speak, or been on Waterloo Station late at night or in the crypt of St Botolph's, Aldgate for the nightly supper, or visited the night shelter in Oxford, will know something of continuing need.

We in the United Kingdom are becoming aware of the number of derelict houses, boarded up and deteriorating further, which could be reconstructed into habitable homes. Many of us begin to identify ourselves with squatters, some of them desperate to find shelter for their families and others bitter against society and landlords, who take the seemingly non-caring law into their own hands.

How does anyone who cares pray about such situations? It is almost impossible to put one's concern into worded prayers. Christians will remember a saying of Jesus a day or two before he went to his death, 'Inasmuch as you did it (or did it not) unto the least of these my brethren you did it (or did it not) unto me.' St Paul spoke of creation groaning inwardly, 'for we do not know how to pray as we ought, but the Spirit himself intercedes for us with sighs too deep for words' (Rom. 8:26).

A prayer said daily by Mother Teresa of Calcutta has helped many caring people to pray and to act, and the example of her community has inspired or shamed many of us to support its work and begin similar efforts in our own back yards:

Dearest Lord, may I see you today and every day in the person of your sick, and whilst nursing them minister to you. Though you hide yourself behind the unattractive disguise of the irritable, the exacting, the unreasonable, may I still recognize you and say: 'Jesus, my patient, how sweet it is to serve you.'

Lord, give me this seeing faith, then my work will never be monotonous. I will ever find joy in humouring the fancies and gratifying the wishes of all poor sufferers.

O beloved sick, how doubly dear you are to me, when you personify Christ; and what a privilege is mine to be allowed to tend you.

Sweetest Lord, make me appreciative of the dignity of my high vocation, and its many responsibilities. Never permit me to disgrace it by giving way to coldness, unkindness, or impatience. And, O God, while you are Jesus, my patient, deign also to be to me a patient Jesus, bearing with my faults, looking only to my intention, which is to love and serve you in the person of each of your sick.

Lord, increase my faith, bless my efforts and work, now and for evermore.

                    Daily prayer of Mother Teresa of Calcutta

Hasten the time, O Lord,
when none of us shall live in contentment

while we know that others have need.
Inspire in us and in people of all nations
the desire for social justice,
that the hungry may be fed,
the homeless welcomed, the sick healed,
and a just order established in the world,
according to thy gracious will
made known in Jesus Christ, our Lord.

G.A.
from *One Man's Prayers*

10

Weep for the World

In the world today there are so many things reported in the media that make one want to weep. Every day we hear of murders, thousands dying of hunger, children dying before they have had a chance to enjoy life, people killed in accidents on our roads or in the air, suicides dying from despair or unbearable pain, political prisoners often under torture, criminals sentenced to long years of imprisonment, in addition to the countless number who die from natural causes or worn out with old age, and the resulting grief of bereavement to their families and friends. Many of us cannot find words to express our grief and concern, except to groan with sighs too deep for words. St Paul spoke of the whole creation groaning in travail together up to his present. But he also spoke of the creation waiting longingly and eagerly for the revealing of the children of God, who would tell the world of God's comforting grace and limitless love.

It is perhaps no wonder that some Christians and many more others put all the suffering down to God, as if he were responsible, punishing people for their sins or failing to intervene on their behalf.

The Isaiah who strengthened the exiles on their return to Jerusalem saw things differently: 'In all their afflictions he was afflicted, and the angel of his presence saved them; in his love and pity he redeemed them; he lifted them up and carried them all the days of old' (Isa. 63:9).

St Luke describes the Messianic entry into Jerusalem:

'And when he drew near and saw the city he wept over it, saying, "Would that even today you knew the things that make for peace! But now they are hid from your eyes' (Luke 19:41–42). Jesus could see what would inevitably happen if the rulers and people in Jerusalem persisted in their unpeaceful ways, and he wept at the war and destruction that would follow.

On the way to Calvary a few days later, when godly women wept helplessly for him, Jesus halted and said to them: 'Daughters of Jerusalem, do not weep for me, but weep for yourselves and your children', for trouble and death would certainly follow.

At a much earlier stage in his ministry, when he was warned of Herod's intention to arrest him after the imprisonment of John the Baptist, Jesus showed his grief over Jerusalem and its treatment of the earlier prophets: 'O Jerusalem, Jerusalem, killing the prophets and stoning them that are sent to you! How often would I have gathered your children together as a hen gathers her brood under her wings, and you would not!' (Matt. 23:37). His warning also shows his love for the city, in the moving and tender picture of a mother hen and her chicks. O Jerusalem, Jerusalem!

A play performed at the Westminster Theatre a few years ago pictures St Columba weeping over the fall of Rome, implicitly suggesting parallels with the state of the world today:

Weep for the world;
How black the night when every light has gone,
How dark the days and months that are to come.

Weep for the world;
Great cities sacked, beloved places burned;
Hope bleeds to death, no staunching of the wound.

Weep for the world;
Mobs rape and kill, and now the fall of Rome;
The beacon light of all the world is gone.

I cannot pray;
When sword is sheathed the plague creeps silently,
My home a grave and day brings tragedy,

O, run and flee,
But where to hide my child? Death stalks the shade,
For Christ has died again and I'm afraid.

My heart is sick;
Hope fails, but in the blackness of despair
Shall flames of faith light up the darkness there,
To light and lead us on?

Juliet Boobbyer and Joanna Sciortino
from *Columba*

Christians cannot leave our meditation at the tragic lament
of the poem quoted, but extrapolate one of our Lord's beati-
tudes, 'Blessed are they that mourn (*over the tragedies of
the world*), for they shall be comforted' (*with the gospel
assurances of God's limitless love and his unceasing
forgiveness*).

> *The sins of the world*
> The sins of the world,
>   such dreadful sins,
>   not just the personal sins
>   but the solidarity of sin,
>   greater than the total
>   of individual sins,
>   nuclear evil in endless fission,
>   O Lamb of God.
>
> The sin of racial pride
>   that sees not the faith
>   that all men are divinely made
>   nor the riches of pigment
>   in portrait faces,

the same psychology
and religious search,
that each is the sibling
    for whom Christ died.

The burgeoning greed
    that never heeds the need of others
    involved in a merciless system,
    looking only at profit and dividend,
    the lust of possessions
        that cannot accompany us
        at our last migration:
Take away these sins,
O Lamb of God.

The massive sin of war,
    millions of lives impersonally destroyed,
    trillions of pounds wasted
    on weapons, bombs,
    truth enslaved,
    the hungry still unfed,
    grief stalking unnumbered homes:
Weep over us,
O Lamb of God.

G.A.
from *The Word is the Seed*

Pope John Paul II at Hiroshima
To you, Creator of nature and humanity, of truth and beauty
I pray:

Hear my voice, for it is the voice of the victims of all wars
and violence among individuals and nations.

Hear my voice, for it is the voice of all children who suffer
and will suffer when people put their faith in weapons and
war.

Hear my voice when I beg you to instil into the hearts of all human beings the wisdom of peace, the strength of justice and the joy of fellowship.

Hear my voice, for I speak for the multitudes in every country and in every period of history who do not want war and are ready to walk the road of peace.

Hear my voice and grant insight and strength so that we may always respond to hatred with love, to injustice with total dedication to justice, to need with the sharing of self, to war with peace.

O God, hear my voice and grant unto the world your ever-lasting peace.

11

Troubled Families

It was recently reported that in 1986 there were 179,844 divorces in the United Kingdom, and this was said to be a welcome 6 per cent fall on the figures for the previous year. That figure meant that 360,000 people had failed in the most personal and intimate relationship in human life. It is easy to be judgmental about such tragedies, but they also evoke a feeling of compassion, for they must leave an emotional scar for the rest of the lives of those involved. Such breakdowns must also bring trouble and problems to any children of these marriages.

The question arises what is to be done when there is no love left in the relationship and there seems no hope of recovering it. Quite a number of couples delay parting until the children have grown up and are able to make their own future. It is always a problem how often each partner wants to have the care of the younger children, at the same time giving the right to the other partner to see them regularly and even to have them to stay in holiday periods.

An even more difficult adjustment arises when one or both divorced persons get married again. The step-parent and step-child relationship is difficult for both, and there needs to be acceptance on both sides. The new spouse may reject the partner's earlier children and vice versa.

Another problematical situation arises in one-parent families, where one parent has to provide the protective care and livelihood as well as the loving assurance that children need, which is only complete in the trinitarian pattern of family life – father, mother and children. Many of the children in the church school of which I was chairman in East London wore a string round the neck with a key on it, so that the child could get into the home if the mother was away doing a job until later.

Children in poor homes like to have the same luxuries as others – new clothes, the same pocket money, the daily visit to the tuck shop, the same children's books. There is an opportunity here for aunts and uncles, and thoughtful neighbours, to take the part of fairy godmothers, though I do not remember as many elfin godfathers in my own youth.

In the marriages which take place in church the priest, after mutual promises from the bride and bridegroom, seals the mutual self-giving with the words, 'Those whom God has joined together let no man put asunder.' The basic question is whether or not it was God who joined them together or sexual attraction or desire for a white wedding in church.

In our present age many parish clergy invite couples who want to be married to a period of preparation before the church wedding, and there are marriage counsellors to help sort out the difficulties which come when being in love is deepening into something more tender and permanently loving.

> *A wedding blessing*
> May the God who is Love
>   eternally loving
>   Bless you both
>   and keep you sweethearts
>   As you give yourselves
>   to each other in love
>   And go through life together
>   in ever-growing tenderness
>   Until you come hand in hand
>   to the joyful mystery of Love –

of Love eternal and divine –
May the God of Love
bless you both
with Love unending.

St Paul assured the Christians in and around Ephesus that
he prayed for them, as he was grateful for their prayers for
him in the sufferings he had incurred on their behalf:

This, then, is what I pray, kneeling before the Father,
from whom every family, whether spiritual or natural,
takes its name: Out of his infinite glory, may he give you
the power through his Spirit for your hidden self to grow
strong, so that Christ may live in your hearts through
faith, and then, planted in love and built on love, you will
with all the saints have strength to grasp the breadth and
the length, the height and the depth; until, knowing the
love of Christ, which is beyond all knowledge, you are
filled with the utter fullness of God. (Eph. 3:14–19; Jerusalem Bible)

Not just Christian families, but every family, spiritual or
natural, some on earth and some already in the heavenly
sphere, every family with members still here and already
there, some who already know God as the original, universal
and eternal Parent, and some who have yet to know that
joyful fact.

12

Cruelty to Children

Many of us who are growing old can remember a reproof from our childhood days, 'children should be seen and not heard', spoken when we joined in the conversation of our elders and betters. If we received nothing worse than that snub we were fortunate, compared with the awful cruelties inflicted on some children today. The story of little Kimberley, barely five years old, cruelly beaten by her mother and lover, shut up in a cold lavatory all night and wanting to die, and finally so injured that she did die, has not only shocked people but has reduced many to tears.

That cruelty has brought news of the overwork of the National Society of Prevention of Cruelty to Children, whose task and financial resources have been stretched to the uttermost. More troubling still, the BBC Childwatch has revealed that many children are still suffering from sexual abuse. We may get a clue to the cause of child cruelty from a consideration of sexual frustration. It has been said that sexual intercourse is the only luxury available for very poor people. If the man is unemployed or has no congenial work or other means of enjoyment, and if at the same time the woman is worried and overtired with lively children to provide food and clothing for and the toys and little luxuries that the children of better-off families enjoy, and is just too worn out for sex, then both feel frustrated and take it out on the apparent cause. Often the nearness of the pub or the off-licence must suggest a break, resulting in children being left alone late at night. Lack of discipline in contraception may result in unwanted and unplanned pregnancies.

We are becoming aware of the various forms of child cruelty – neglect, lack of love, psychological cruelty, physical suffering, sexual abuse – that leave their effects on the rest of life. I remember at a retreat I was conducting, a quite elderly woman told me that she could never use the word Father for God because she had been frequently interfered with sexually by her own father. She was overjoyed to learn of the word Jesus often used, 'Abba', the familiar name which children in a Jewish home today still use for their father, conveying the warmth and affection of 'father, dear father'.

Photographs in the press and moving TV clips of starving children in Somalia, the Sudan, Ethiopia and other places wring the heart, as do the emaciated mothers with empty breasts and despairing faces, hopelessly waiting for the relief that is so slow in coming. One can only groan and agitate for the massive help that our nations and political parties should be willing to give, to be ministered in the pattern way that voluntary societies work. One almost wishes to be a vandal and scrawl '.7%' all over the place, with exclamation and question marks galore.

For Christians our Lord had some imperative things to say. 'Let the little ones come,' he said to his disciples who thought he should not be bothered. With a little child happily sitting on his knee with his arm lovingly in support, he taught the crowd that in the kingdom of God we must become as trusting, humble and eager to learn as unspoilt children are.

There was a stern warning to anyone who causes children to stumble or sin: 'it would be better for him to have a great millstone fastened round his neck and to be drowned in the depth of the sea' (Luke 17:2). I do not think that was a threat of what God would do to such offenders but a warning to every one of his dismay and horror when he realised the extent of the damage he was causing.

There is a lovely picture in the book of Zechariah (8:4–5) of exiles returning to Jerusalem rebuilt and at peace: 'Old men and old women shall again sit in the streets of Jerusalem with a staff (*walking stick*) in hand for very age. And the streets of the city shall be full of boys and girls playing (*safely*) in the streets'. Such a text reminds us that women and children suffer first and most when war breaks out. It is also relevant to city planners and all involved in the reconstruction of the decayed and neglected inner cities, and in their repair of slum property.

Child sufferers

O God, our Father, we remember before Thee all orphaned, homeless and unwanted children, the children of loveless homes, and those who suffer from bodily defect and disease. Make our hearts burn within us for the children of our dark places, and teach us how to turn to good account the laws that protect them and the efforts of those who strive to succour them; through Jesus Christ our Lord.

Mothers' Union
from F. B. MacNutt, *The Prayer Manual*

Loving hands

Jesus' hands were kind hands, doing good to all;
Healing pain and sickness, blessing children small;
Washing tired feet, and saving those who fall;
Jesus' hands were kind hands, doing good to all.

Take my hands, Lord Jesus, let them work for you.
Make them strong and gentle, kind in all I do;
Let me watch you, Jesus, till I'm gentle too,
Till my hands are kind hands, quick to work for you.

Margaret Cropper

God's care
God who made the earth,
The air, the sky, the sea,
He who gave the light its birth,
and cares for me.

God, who made the grass,
The flower, the fruit, the tree,
The day and night to pass,
Cares too for me.

God who made the sun,
The moon, the stars, is He
Who, when life's clouds come on,
Still cares for me.

Sarah Betts Rhodes
from *Songs of Praise*

The childlike heart
Grant me, O God,
the heart of a child,
pure and transparent as a spring;
   a simple heart,
which never harbours sorrows;
a heart glorious in self-giving,
   tender in compassion;
a heart faithful and generous,
which will never forget any good.
or bear a grudge for any evil.

   Make me a heart gentle and humble,
   loving without asking any return,
   largehearted and undauntable,
which no ingratitude can sour
and no indifference can weary;
   a heart penetrated by the love of Jesus
   whose desire will only be
   satisfied in heaven.

Grant me, O Lord,
the mind and heart
of thy dear Son.

G.A.
from *One Man's Prayers*

13

Crowded Prisons

The number of people in British prisons has passed the 50,000 mark. New prisons are being built, old prisons renovated, the humiliating insanitary conditions being done away with; non-harming offenders are having their offences examined to see if fines and suspended sentences are more appropriate and remedial; the possibility of parole is being periodically considered, capital punishment abolished, physical punishment lessened, solitary confinement questioned, and discussion groups organised. While the figures of violence and the growing number of burglaries and muggings cannot but be deplored, there are factors for which to be thankful.

Society must be protected, especially the old and the lonely and children. Massive police hunts and crime watch activities make detection and arrest more probable. Organised drug trade demands international control, and drug addicts and alcoholics are offered treatment.

More and more the causes of crimes are being tackled, the need of arousing conscience, the recognition of the spiritual element in personality, the availability of psychiatric treatment, the appointment of prison visitors and the ministry of prison chaplains are seen as curative possibilities.

Having visited prisons in different parts of the world I realise the need of compassion, both for the victims of fraud and violence and those who are sentenced to terms of imprisonment. There are people who demand heavier sentences, but I, as a Christian, try to put myself in the position of one

sentenced to a long term and imagine the despair of the first
night in prison and the bleakness of the years ahead. I hope
that prayer may in the providence of God help towards
empathy, penitence and the grace to grow into what God
plans each individual to be. I try to think of prayer as an
isosceles triangle of the relationship of God, the person
prayed for, and the person praying, with the faith that stone
walls and iron bars cannot keep out the presence of God in
his compassion and forgiveness.

In his sermon at Nazareth after the experience of his
baptism and his forty days retreat in the Jericho countryside,
Jesus outlined what he saw to be his vocation:

> The Spirit of the Lord is upon me, because he has anointed
> me to preach good news to the poor. He has sent me to
> proclaim release to the captives and recovering of sight to
> the blind, to set at liberty those who are oppressed, to
> proclaim the acceptable year of the Lord. (Luke 4:18–19)

His own acceptance of this vocation, his dedication to it and
his assurance of God's anointing power to carry it out are
seen in a later verse, 'Today this scripture is fulfilled in your
ears.' The scripture which Jesus read in the synagogue at
Nazareth was from the opening words of Isaiah 61. It is
significant to note that he finished his quotation before the
minatory words 'and the day of vengeance of our God'.
It is equally interesting to read Luke's comment on the
congregation's reception. 'And all spoke well of him, and
wondered at the gracious words which proceeded out of his
mouth' (4:22).

The relevance to this meditation is his reference to prisons
and prisoners. 'He has sent me to proclaim release to the
captives.' For there are many spiritual prisons in which we
shut ourselves up – fear, anxieties, rigidities, resentments,
hatreds, envyings, uncharitable attitudes and judgments,
pride and selfish motives. The Holy Spirit can reveal these

sinful failings, and remind us of our Lord's promise 'If you continue in my word, you are truly my disciples . . . and the truth will make you free' (John 8:31–32).

There is a great responsibility of religious bodies to work for moral welfare which will save people in every locality and nation from harming others, and to act in such a way that they will not engage in anti-social activities. There are subtle temptations in such efforts. One is the idea that the thing to be avoided is being found out rather than the commission of a crime. A deeper one is that one's nature and character are fixed and cannot be changed, and so one should not be held responsible. It is at this point that the spiritual factor comes in, both in honest self-knowledge, and in the acceptance of grace and forgiveness. We who recognise this obligation must not feel that to preach it is sufficient, but submit to it and show the effects on our own character and activities, without self-righteous claims.

These considerations should also inspire our prayer, being thankful for protective police, caring probation officers and dutiful social workers, and praying for all people we know personally that they may be guided and sustained in their difficult tasks. Nor must we forget to pray for our politicians, who make the decisions and decide the conditions for operation, and in the end have to raise the money by fixing adequate and acceptable levels of taxation.

The level of crime and overcrowded prisons are evidence that the churches, especially the Church of England, which claims to be a national church, are failing in their responsibility for the moral welfare of the nation. The general confession in morning and evening prayer in the 1662 Book of Common Prayer is not designed only for individual penitence, but for the corporate failures of congregations, and the failure of a whole denomination and the churches. Perhaps there should be a two-minute silence before our general confession, and a two-minute silence afterwards of heartfelt gratitude for God's forgiveness and the first prayer

of Jesus on the cross: 'Father, forgive them, for they know
not what they do'; and the earlier assurance, 'God sent not
his Son into the world to condemn the world, but that the
world through him might be saved.' Saved from what? Saved
from sinning, the guilt of the past, and refusal of grace for
the future.

The following prayers, should be prayed slowly, with
conscious-stricken memory and penitent hearts:

> Most gracious Father, we humbly beseech Thee for thy
> Holy Catholic Church. Fill it with all truth; in all truth
> with all peace. Where it is corrupt, purge it; where it is
> in error, direct it; where anything is amiss, reform it;
> where it is right, strengthen and confirm it; where it is in
> want, furnish it; where it is divided and rent asunder,
> make up the breaches of it, O Thou Holy One of Israel.
>
> Archbishop William Laud (1573–1645)

For governors, warders and magistrates
O Holy Spirit of God, inspire with thy wisdom and love
those set in chief authority over prisoners; teach them so
to rule with mercy and with justice, neither despising nor
neglecting their brethren whom Thou hast put under their
care, that they may show forth the Spirit in which Thou
dost rule and judge the hearts of men; through Jesus
Christ our Saviour.

Guild of SS Paul and Silas, 1881
from Selina Fitzherbert Fox, *A Chain of Prayer*
Across the Ages

For spiritual work in prisons
O Lord Jesus Christ, the Great Shepherd of the sheep,
who seekest those that are gone astray, bindest up those
that are broken, and healest those that are sick; bless, we
beseech Thee, the efforts made in prisons to convert souls
unto Thee. Open the deaf ears of the wanderers, that they

may hear the words which belong unto their salvation; and grant that those whom Thou dost raise into newness of life may, through thy grace, persevere unto the end, for thy honour and glory.

(ibid.)

14

More Old People

People in Britain do not need to be very old to notice that there are many more old people than there seemed to be even a few years ago. This is due to better medical care and to more medical research into the cure and care of sick people. The acceptance of the welfare state is also a creative factor. Age does make us aware of the growing diminishments and disabilities of old people, and the pain of bereavement when a lifelong partner dies leaving the survivor lonely and sad.

I often wish that Jesus had lived to old age so that he could have shown us how to adjust to it, and how families, friends, neighbours and church people could help to make it enjoyable. Jesus was observant, as we see in his warning to Simon Peter: 'Truly, I say to you, when you were young, you dressed yourself and walked where you would; but when you are old you will stretch out your hands, and another will dress you and carry you where you do not wish to go' (John 21:18). We can be sure that with his love for the book of Isaiah Jesus would have known 46:3–4: 'You have been borne by me from your birth, carried from the womb; even to your old age I am he, and to gray hairs I will carry you. I have made and I will bear; I will carry and will save'.

Fairly old people now have to accept early retirement, with its problems and opportunities, the realisation that younger people have the responsibility, authority and leadership that we older ones once had. We have to accept this willingly and gracefully, not for ever telling our successors what they ought to do, yet taking an interest in what they are doing and planning.

We can grow old grudgingly or graciously. A kindly parish priest getting on in years lamented what he called 'the tragedy of our times', that while there are many ageing beings there are few who are genuinely old and wise: 'We expect serenity and peace from the old, but instead they are touchy, irritable and fussy, a constant burden to patient relatives who look after them.' Another elderly priest speaks of the serene presence and detachment that transforms everything around them. I have noticed (and experienced) the happy relationship that often exists between grandparents and grandchildren. Parents tend to be preoccupied in making a livelihood and running the home, and do not have as much time as they would wish in deepening the relationship with their children. Grandparents have more time at their disposal.

Yet there are many lonely people, often living alone and growing less able to cope with life. They need almost daily contacts and warm friendship. Here the telephone can be a blessing. Perhaps the time will come when every lonely pensioner will be provided with the phone, and be expected to pay for calls only, and even there the calling-up charge might well be borne by the younger and perhaps better-off relative or friend.

Old age may also be a time for crossing the frontier between this life and the next in memory and prayer, as well as a time of preparation for our last migration, where we can get a foretaste of the eternal which God has prepared for them that love him and, faith would add, for those who do not yet do so because they have not seen the divine love at work in those who say they believe in him.

The Church ought to be the community that takes the initiative in this care for the old and lonely, for the Anglican

Church has no less that 10,000 parishes, and Christians of other churches could well double this number.

Prayers that may help us:

Growing old
Lord, I am growing old. I am slower than I used to be. My memory is not so good. The disabilities and irritations of old age come upon me. I find myself telling the same old jokes. Loved ones and friends pass on across the frontier of this life and the next. Lord God, I dare to ask if in prayer I may keep in touch with them and they with me. May your beloved Son, who brings love to us, take our love to them, for he still spans this world of creation and the world of full life, joy and blessing, O Love, Eternal and Boundless.

G.A.

In the autumn
Heavenly Father, in the autumn of nature the ageing leaves are touched with gold. Give us grace that in the autumn of life there may be a touch of beauty and colour. Help us to be fully open to the winter not far ahead, knowing that our souls will be warmed by your love, and gathered into the home that your Son, in your divine providence, is preparing for all who love him, and for those who do not yet know him but will do so when he welcomes them to the eternal home of your will. Blessed be You for ever!

G.A.

15

The Vocabulary of Death

As a priest I have ministered at many funerals, been present at deathbeds, been the confidant of people's fear of death, and tried to comfort bereaved relatives and friends. For many years too I have been troubled by the words we use about those who have died, and the words used in expressions of sympathy, in media reports, memorial tributes and reports of funerals.

Our way of speaking often seems to suggest too close an identification of the person with the dead body. The notices end with the statement that he or she was buried at such-and-such a cemetery or was cremated at a neighbouring crematorium. Religious faith should surely speak of the body, the mortal remains being reverently disposed of.

The physical presence and characteristics are understandably remembered first, and then our experience of relationship, the kind of person he or she was, as we recollect in memory and gratitude, waiting for the corpse to be brought solemnly into the chapel.

In former funeral services the words 'in the midst of life we are in death' were usually included. Faith would surely prefer to say 'in the midst of death we are in life'. The women friends of Jesus who with two Pharisee friends took down the dead limp body from the cross were early at the sepulchre on the morning after the Sabbath. They came away with the assurance, perceived intuitively or spoken by spiritual presences, 'He is not here. He is risen!'

A verse of the English poet Longfellow is worth pondering over, if we go further than the often-quoted first line:

> Life is real! Life is earnest!
>   and the grave is not its goal;
> Dust thou art, to dust returnest,
>   was not spoken to the soul.

No! It is spoken to the body, no longer eager to obey the spirit, as it may have done in earlier years.

I am grateful to a Roman theologian, Ladislaus Boros, for an assurance in his book, *Living in Hope:*

> No one is damned merely by chance, because he was suddenly called to eternity by an accident, or because he was born into a family where he never knew what love is . . . or because he was hated, rejected, misjudged and wounded to the heart by human beings and so rebelled against everything, including God.

Jesus in the moment of excruciating pain as he was nailed to the cross prayed, 'Father, forgive them for they know not what they do,' making excuses for all who had a hand in bringing him there, showing his understanding of the heart of God, who in his eternal mercy and love knows the heart of humans, even if the perception of the divine indwelling is still little more than a seed.

St Paul brings an insight to our wonderings when he speaks not only of death's inevitability, but of its necessity. Flesh and blood, he says, cannot inherit God's spiritual kingdom, the perishable must become immortal. He adds, 'We shall all be changed in a flash, in the twinkling of an eye', suggesting to me that the moment I fall asleep here in this world I begin to live there, that there is an immediate changeover from time to eternity. I enter a new kind of being and live in a new milieu, released from the domination of time, space, distance, and physical eyesight.

In one point I feel and hope that Paul is wrong in speaking of death as 'the last enemy'. I am more grateful to St Francis of Assisi who in his moving *Canticle of the Sun* sang to his guitar, 'Praise be to God, for our kindly sister death.' The real enemy is the fear of death, amounting to distrust in the God of love.

I have often talked with friends and colleagues about my own search for the right word in speaking of those who have 'died'. Some have suggested 'the risen ones' and this certainly implies a presence not perceptible to physical sight. Popular journalese speaks of 'the departed one'; my hope and faith would prefer 'the arrived one', but that would suggest a going away from here and an arrival somewhere else. The 'late lamented' certainly implies regret and grief at what has happened, but is a term I am most reluctant to use. The most acceptable term so far is 'the risen ones', which suggests that they are still living and in a new order of being, a new milieu, with a new type of communication not limited to physical touch and sight, not earthbound or confined to past memory.

It is understandable that the grave where a loved one's mortal remains are buried should be kept in good order and on anniversaries or seasons of the year honoured with flowers and plants. Equally one understands an organised visit to the war cemeteries kept in such good order by the War Graves Commission with individual memorial stones, but would hope for the same intuition that came to the faithful women disciples on the first Easter morning, 'He is not here, he is risen!' We need not a static memory but a dynamic ongoing hope.

We can keep in touch through prayer, the sending of our love to them through the risen Lord who spans this world and the next. It may well be that in the providence of the God of love, the eternal and universal Father, they may

know something of how we fare on earth and be there to
welcome us as we finally cross the frontier.

The following prayers may keep alive this hope and faith:

Father of all, we pray to Thee for those whom we love,
but see no longer. Grant them thy peace; let light
perpetual shine upon them; and in thy loving wisdom and
almighty power work in them the good purpose of thy
perfect will; through Jesus Christ our Lord.

BCP (1928)

O heavenly Father, who in thy Son Jesus Christ has given
us a true faith, and a sure hope: Help us, we pray Thee,
to live as those who believe and trust in the Communion
of Saints, the forgiveness of sins, and the resurrection to
life everlasting, and strengthen this faith and hope in us
all the days of our life: through the love of thy Son, Jesus
Christ our Saviour.

BCP (1928)

God of eternity, whose blessed Son lived in time to show
us the divine and eternal life, so that we serving Thee in
time might learn something of thy divine life and even
now begin to experience the timelessness of heaven: Grant
that being made in your image, time may merge into
eternity, the material into the spiritual, the mortal into
the immortal, faith into sight, so that I may grow into the
spiritual stature and character of your perfect Son and be
finished and complete as you intended me to be at my
spiritual birth.

G.A.
from *Entry into Life*

O God, we thy creatures try to evade the fact of death,
and to keep it out of mind, yet in our deeper moments
we know it is a warning note, urging us so to die every

day to all selfishness and sin, that when the time comes
for our final migration, we may take death in our stride
because life is so strong within us, as it was in him who
was so manifestly thy true Son and so convincingly the
prototype of thy finished humanity, even Jesus Christ, thy
Son, our brother.

G.A.
(ibid.)

16

The Root of Evil

Not money itself, in the thinking of Paul, but the love of money, makes the acquisition of money the main motive in life and the governing principle in planning and way of life. More than once in my personal ministry in different parts of the world when I have reproached someone for what seemed to be a mistaken and selfish action, the reply has been, 'But Father, I couldn't possibly refuse such an offer, could I?' It has been cynically said that everyone has his price, the only difference being that with some the price is higher than with others, that is, that the level of greed is greater.

One of the shortest and disturbing parables of Jesus has come to have the title of 'The Rich Fool'. It is the story of a rich man whose business prospered so continuously that he felt he must pull down his barns and build bigger ones. Then came a night when death threatened and he realised that he could take none of his accumulated wealth with him. Jesus put his warning later in a pithy saying, 'You cannot serve God and mammon', the love of money. It was wiser, in his estimation, to use money for good purposes and so store up the gratitude of people in need, and those who had been helped by generous gifts.

Somehow Paul had picked up a saying of Jesus that no one else in the New Testament had written down: 'Remember the words of the Lord Jesus, how he said, "It is more blessed to give than to receive"?' Both Jesus and

Paul were implying that giving brought greater blessing and happiness than receiving, not just that it was more right. If we have any doubts about the truth of this insight, it would be well worthwhile to try it out.

The advertising pages of our newspapers today are full of exhortations and methods of getting rich quick, and of tempting assurances that if we only follow the experts' advice the future will be safe and bright. Money has got into sport in a big way and tempts players to protest against decisions they do not like, to engage in 'professional fouls' and 'that's not cricket' practices; while some spectators of both sides engage in violent partisanship, to guard against which football clubs, for example, have to spend large sums for police presence and protection.

There is still an 'unacceptable level' of bribery and corruption in many countries and often the people in desperate need do not get the full help that charitable enterprises and overseas aid provide. Perhaps compassionate donors, individual and corporate, may feel that even if only a proportion gets through to the desperate sufferers, we must be thankful. God's will is always for an order in which all may be happy to live free from fear and want, free from harming and being harmed. The snag is that every new generation has to learn this afresh.

The golden calf as the symbol of an idol goes right back to Moses, before he returned from Mount Sinai to the children of Israel, bearing in his heart and mind the laws by which his people, and all God's people, should live. The 'logo' of a golden calf is still sadly not yet out of date.

People today might think they are too sophisticated to worship metal images. Our danger is to idolise the images we set up in our own minds – images of God, ourselves, worldly patterns, trendish fashions – and give to any of them a priority or imperative which should be given to God alone, admitting that our highest conceptions always fall short of

the perfection of God and our behaviour woefully short of
his righteousness, holiness and love.

Help us, O Lord, to understand the place of money in
our life. Keep before us the peril of loving it. Help us to
make it our servant, never our master. And let not the
lack of it loose our grasp upon the true riches which are
ours through the grace of Jesus Christ our Lord.

Dick Williams

Guard us, O Lord, from the wrong use of money:
   from selfishness, carelessness, or waste
and from that obsessive love of money
   which is a root of all evils.
Enable us to be good stewards
   of what is entrusted to us
to give or spend or save according to your will;
so that neither poverty nor wealth
   may hinder our discipleship,
   harm our neighbours,
   or destroy our life;
We offer this prayer through Jesus Christ, our Lord.

Christopher Idle

We pray, O God, for those whose lives
are immersed day by day
   in the busy and complex work of commerce,
with its many demands, responsibilities
   and temptations.
Save them from being so absorbed
   in material wealth
that they lose sight of the things
   of priceless value,
the things that are worth more
   than all the money in the world.
Give them integrity of character,

that their lives may be sincere,
   their dealings honest,
   and their words truthful;
We ask this in the name of Christ,
   the Lord of all life.

Frank Colquhoun

all from *More Parish Prayers*, ed. Canon Colquhoun

17

Unemployment

Three million unemployed in the depression of the 1930s, which followed the First World War; three million unemployed in the 1980s in the aftermath of the Second World War. This is another figure that ought to be engraved on the conscience of everyone who accepts the two great commandments of the eternal God, endorsed by one whose sole purpose was to be the obedient loving Son of the Father of all and therefore the universal brother to all. How do we his disciples today pray about this awful fact, this dreadful figure, this disaster, this tragedy, and yet this challenge.

First we need to tell the eternal God (and others) that we know that this is not his will, that he is at work to oppose it, and to ask him to give us the wisdom of inspiration to change it.

Secondly we need to feel the pain and hopelessness in the hearts of each of that vast crowd of sufferers, to put ourselves in their place, to wear their shoes, those who have shoes of some sort and those who have no shoes for themselves and more poignantly for their children.

So our first prayer must be 'Thy will be done', not in resignation, as we often think of it, but in glad excitement that there is an eternal purpose at work, renewed in every generation, working for a new order of compassion, if we will let him rule in human hearts and human affairs, so that the world may be a happy place in which to live.

Certain essentials are being seen for happy human living.

The first is the dutiful doing of the chores in society, what is paid for and voluntarily performed. This gives the doer a sense of satisfaction, as well as benefiting others. Then it is necessary that every person should receive sufficient to survive, with a little over for emergencies. Thirdly there is the need to meet others and perhaps co-operate with them in seizing some opportunity; and underlying it all the need to be treated as a person, rather than the mechanical carrying out of a prescribed bureaucratic procedure.

All these essentials involve spiritual values and the acknowledgement of a transcendent principle, a responsibility for human rights and an answerability to God for the well-being of one's neighbour.

There are positive factors in this problem of unemployment. A great deal of hard labour and indeed very skilled labour is now being done by machines, which need fewer operators and less time. We can all have much more time for leisure, for enjoyment of family life and the pursuit of hobbies.

When a writer in *The Times* recently spoke of the few jobs available, especially for the unskilled, he also spoke of the depressing effect of continued failure to find work:

> Most of those who find work, find it within the first three months of unemployment. The problem is much worse for those who have been unemployed for longer than a year. Their opinion of themselves often becomes so low that when they do apply for a job their depressed bearing militates against them.

He went on to speak of the need of some order in life and the weakening effect of not having some self-discipline: 'The unemployed person who neglects order, rises at midday and drifts aimlessly without focus or pattern, is in danger of falling apart.'

The accusing figure of three million is slowly decreasing,

but will never get significantly reduced in our present economic order. Can we hope for shorter working shifts, possibly for an extra shift each day and with targets of efficiency and production accepted, and overtime avoided except in the cases of emergency? It would need agreed adjustment in wages, with some bonus for reaching the target and a reduction in overtime. Ultimately we may have one or more representatives of the workers on the management, chosen from the workers in a particular firm, and not appointed by an outside body.

Once again the solution of problems is a spiritual one, demanding joint consideration and mutual goodwill. The following prayers, said thoughtfully and slowly, and repeatedly, may reveal possibilities as yet unperceived. Prayer helps to keep God in each situation, with his justice, love and wisdom:

O Lord and heavenly Father, we commend to thy care and protection the men and women of this land who are suffering distress and anxiety through lack of work. Strengthen and support them, we beseech Thee; and so prosper the counsels of those who govern and direct our industries, that thy people may be set free from want and fear to work in peace and security, for the relief of their necessities and the well-being of this realm; through Jesus Christ our Lord.

F. B. MacNutt
Industrial Christian Fellowship

Guide us, O Lord, amidst the trials and conflicts of our social life, and fill our centres of industry with thy presence; that daily work may become to us a high vocation, and that all may learn the dignity of labour and make it a freewill offering to Thee; through Jesus Christ our Lord.
Anon.

O blessed Savour, who wast pleased thyself to be numbered among the craftsmen: we pray Thee to guide and prosper all who labour with mind and hand, that their work may be done for thine honour and rewarded with thine approval and the gratitude of consumers; who livest and reignest with the Father and the Holy Spirit, one God, world without end.

Anon.

all from F. B. MacNutt, *The Prayer Manual*

18

Homes for All

In 1948 the General Assembly of the United Nations adopted a Universal Declaration of Human Rights which set out a number of rights, economic, cultural and political, to be a standard of human rights which it was hoped that all member nations would accept and put into practice. Among them, implied or specifically mentioned, was the right of all to secure and decent housing. The year 1987 was designated as the International Year of Shelter for the Homeless and as the year ended the provision of Christmas cheer over an extended period brought relief and enjoyment to many homeless people, and a stirring of conscience to many already enjoying comfortable and happy homes.

In the United Kingdom Cardinal Basil Hume is the President of the registered charity Shelter, and Archbishop John Habgood recently made an appeal on its behalf:

It is a shocking fact that last year in Britain – one of the wealthiest countries in the world – over 100,000 households were officially registered as being homeless. A further 203,000 mostly single people and couples without children, who applied to local authorities to be registered, do not qualify under present regulations to be included in the official figures of homelessness. Nor is that all: there are still further tens of thousands currently living in overcrowded or unsuitable accommodation – the majority of them are elderly people and those on low incomes. The young and the old are particularly hard hit by our worsening national housing problem.

The Archbishop and his colleagues in Shelter calculated that at a cost of £208 it was possible to find a secure home for some homeless family, and pleaded that decent housing should be accepted as a fundamental right for all.

The situation in the United Kingdom is shocking enough, but there is even greater need in many other countries. Mother Teresa has made known to the world the desperate need in Calcutta, where many sleep on the streets and every night a distressing number die. In Cairo many homeless people find shelter in the tombs section of the city. Television has made us aware of the vast number of homeless people who have fled from famine areas in African countries and for whom urgent relief is prevented or delayed by internal divisions. Palestinians with their attachment to the stone cottages and little plots of land need to be assured of continuing possession. Jews longing for a safe homeland after centuries of exile sometimes forget that Arabs are also descendants of Abraham, father of Ishmael and Isaac. Surely these two forms of love of home and land are not incompatible.

The following quotation from *Faith in the City* was included in a Christmas service of Shelter:

In Britain today there is a shortage of good-quality secure homes to rent for those who have no chance to buy. Phrases like 'housing crisis' recur in newspaper headlines; what is less commonly recognised is the hardship which such headlines represent. Millions of people are suffering because they do not have a place which they recognise as home.

The Church's commitment to the values of the Kingdom is a vision that is rooted in justice for those who suffer; and it is precisely because we have seen so much suffering in the urban priority areas that we believe that the Church must state firmly and clearly that the present situation is unacceptable. The poor have a right to a home, which does not depend on their ability to pay. This must be the starting point. Only when this fact is acknowledged can the nation begin to act, there is no time to lose. The situation we face is urgent.

The time has come for decent secure housing to be accepted as a fundamental right for all.

We Christians who celebrate each Christmas the coming of one for whom there was no room in the caravanserai at Bethlehem, so that his mother had to give birth in a stable and lay her child in a manger, must have a deep compassion for those for whom there is no room in the inn of the world.

Ezekiel, who looked forward to an age of peace and jubilee inaugurated by a divine messenger, spoke of a time when God would give his people a new heart, no longer one of stone, but a heart of flesh, with truly human feelings and a new spirit which would inspire them to keep his laws (Ezek. 36:26–27), to love God with all one's heart, mind and will (Deut. 6:4–9), and to love one's neighbour as oneself (Lev. 19:17–18, 33–34).

St Paul describes the new heart for Christians: 'If anyone is in Christ, he is a new creation' (2 Cor. 5:17). The true disciple is a new person, living in a new milieu, having Christ's mind for himself and the world, and doing everything in his power to aid God in his creation of the world of his will.

We are told that 500 million people still live in slums and shanty towns. In the 1930s C. Day Lewis wrote two bitter stanzas which move the hearts of all whose hearts are no longer as hard as stone.

> O hush thee, my baby,
> Thy cradle's in pawn:

No blankets to cover thee
Cold and forlorn.
The stars in the bright sky
Look down and are dumb
At the heir of the ages
Asleep in a slum.

The hooters are blowing,
No heed let him take;
When baby is hungry
'Tis best not to wake.
Thy mother is crying,
Thy dad's on the dole:
Two shillings a week
Is the price of a soul.

A Carol

Let us thank God for his loving will and unceasing purposes.

O God, I thank thee that thy will is love instead of hatred, health instead of disease, life instead of death, plenty instead of hunger, peace instead of war, freedom instead of oppression, decent houses instead of slums, caring communities instead of concentration camps, refugee camps, prisons, heaven instead of hell. I know that thou wilt never cease thy eternal purpose of love until thy Kingdom comes on earth as in heaven, and thy will be done by men as well as by angels and saints. Blessed be thou, good God!

G.A.
from *Journey for a Soul*

19

Health for All

The twentieth century may well be remembered and judged, not only for the discovery of nuclear energy and its destructive misuse, not only for the amazing development of communication through air lines flying faster than sound, radio and television, not only for the hope of peace through the United Nations Organisation, but also for the marked improvement in health. In healing when health breaks down, epidemics spread, accidents take place, and psychiatry is called in on the mental breakdowns that seem more frequent than in the past, the development of national health and social services helps create the conditions in which all may live happily and securely. Those of us humans with religious convictions must be heartfelt in our thanksgiving for such welcome developments in individual care and in the operation of the World Health Organisation.

We can be thankful also for the conviction that God is a God of love, who does not inflict disease and tragedy on mankind, either by punishment or with the aim of bringing humans to our senses. We can be equally sure that in everything negative or tragic our loving God is always at work to redeem the situation, to turn tragedy into blessing, to forgive the mistakes, muddles, ignorance and deliberate ill-will that result in so many unhappy consequences. We can only make that forgiveness effective by changing our thinking and behaviour, accepting his supporting grace and guidance in the future. All this can only happen if we keep in touch by thought, prayer and meditation with the God who is perfect in holiness and love, unceasingly forgiving and abundantly generous, always and everywhere at work on his eternal plan of saving love. Jesus in the gospels speaks of being made whole, of becoming a whole personality of spirit, mind and body, all or any of which needs healing. Peter in his courageous visit and sharing a meal in the house of a Roman centurian Cornelius, says of Jesus, 'he went about doing good and healing all that were oppressed by the devil, for God was with him' (Acts 10:38). Here, as so often in the gospels, the priority of healing the spirit is stressed, whether of a mentally disturbed person in the synagogue (Mark 9:21–26), the man paralysed by guilt (Mark 2:1–12) or the raving lunatic in the Gerasene countryside (Mark 5:1–20).

In this last encounter I picture Jesus, quietly unafraid sitting down by the demented man, and as the outbursts quietened asking him, 'What is your name?' thus recalling him to his forgotten self. The man's bitter answer 'My name is Legion; for we are many', suggests that he felt torn in a multi-schizophrenia. The only point that bothers me is the assumption that Jesus sent the devils into the great herd of swine feeding near, a more acceptable interpretation being that the swine became frightened by the raving shouts of the man and fled down the steep bank into the sea. The main point of the incident is that the quiet friendly contact with Jesus was something he had not experienced with relatives and village leaders trying to chain him up with a violence stronger than his own.

If the spirit, the core or heart of personality, is healed there is an in-flow of spiritual health and loving grace which will affect mind and body, inspiring new attitudes and wise ways of living, and a conscious relationship with God whose will is health, healing and happiness.

Anyone who studies critically the gospels and the interpretation of other writers in the New Testament can have little doubt that Jesus had the gift of physical as well as spiritual healing. Touched by even the finger of God, many who looked to him in appeal and faith became healed.

There are 'faith healers' today who seem to have the gift of permanent healing. Some of them, with their publicity and their appeals for money, seem to forget that they are channels of healing and are tempted to thinking of their possession of the gift.

The connection between body, mind and spirit, the 'psychosomatic' element, is seen in experiments carried out by doctors, psychologists, clergy and laboratory technicians in America and Japan. They have examined the effect of prayerful meditation on output of brain energy, breath rate, heart beat and blood pressure. They have discovered that oxygen consumption decreases by up to 20 per cent after three minutes quiet meditation, a result that takes five hours of sleep to achieve; the rate of heart beat decreases; breathing rate slows down; with continuous discipline blood pressure becomes lower; the blood lactate which is associated with anxiety decreases.

All this may seem very humanistic and empirical, utilitarian even, yet authenticating the spiritual element of our personality and driving us back to God, the source, the power at work within life, the love at the heart of things.

Sickness of heart brought about by spiritual causes can only be cured by spiritual means. Life integrated in God, guarded in peace by our trust in him, refreshed and renewed by our touch with him, sense of guilt set right by the acceptance of God's forgiveness, can all help towards the abundant life which is his will for everyone.

Meditation on this matter has led me into quiet communion expressed in the following prayer:

O Spirit of God, set at rest the crowded, hurrying anxious thoughts within our minds and hearts. Let the peace and quiet of thy presence take possession of us. Help us to rest, to relax, to become open and receptive to Thee. Thou dost know our inmost spirits, the hidden unconscious life within us, the forgotten memories of hurts and fears, the frustrated desires, the unresolved tensions and dilemmas. Cleanse and sweeten the springs of our being, that freedom, life and love may flow into both our conscious and hidden life. Lord, we lie open before Thee, waiting for thy peace, thy healing, and thy word.

G.A.
from *Jerusalem Prayers*

The mind of the believer in God is troubled by other considerations. On the roads of Britain 600 people are said to die in motor accidents every month, and several times as many are injured. Many of these accidents are due to rash driving, or driving under the influence of alcohol. 'One for the road' is a thoughtless and dangerous invitation, amounting to tempting guests of our hospitality. Fortunately appeals and warnings on radio and TV are being effective, as well as perhaps the haunting memory of having caused the death or injury of others on the road.

A prayer prayed and written by Bishop Douglas Crick of Chester in Road Safety Week 1949 could well be quoted regularly in the publications of the AA and RAC:

Almighty God, giver of life and health, guide, we pray Thee, with thy wisdom all who are striving to save from injury and death the travellers on our roads. Grant to those who drive along the highways consideration for others, and to those who walk on them or play beside them thoughtful caution and care; that so without fear or disaster we all may come safely to our journeys' ends, by thy mercy who carest for us; through Jesus Christ our Lord.

from F. B. MacNutt *The Prayer Manual*

A further troubling matter is that of diseases at present incurable. Chief among these is the incidence of cancer. Here again there are many researchers working to discover the cause, which may lead quickly to its cure. There are other diseases like multiple sclerosis and motor neurone disease. Perhaps the most troubling of present infectious incurable diseases is that of AIDS, so easily transmitted by promiscuity or infected blood. A paragraph written by Mother Jane of the Sisters of the Love of God in Oxford is one that has enlightened and comforted me:

If He were a vindictive authority figure who, for instance, strikes a promiscuous society with the scourge of AIDS, God would hardly bother to be born as a baby. The message of Christmas is that he yearns for us to turn to Him freely and lovingly. He shows us through the Incarnation the amazing truth that He is us and we are Him, and that nothing 'in all creation, will be able to separate us from the love of God in Christ Jesus our Lord' (Rom. 8:39). God is at one with every man, woman and child dying of AIDS; with the victims of all violence, accidents and natural disasters; with drug pushers, arms dealers, child molesters and the perpetrators of all the terrible outrages we hear of constantly. He is at one with those who rise in the midst of catastrophes to heights of heroism, and with those who don't.

from *Fairacres Chronicle* (Winter 1987)

For people of spiritual search and faith the question of suicides is another troubling problem. It is calculated that more than 1000 people in the world commit suicide every day. This is presumably a global estimate. It is good that suicide is no longer regarded as a crime, and that the refusal to bury the bodies of suicides in consecrated ground is not insisted upon. Such a death is a tragedy whatever the reason for it – shame, despair, no incentive for living, unbearable pain, or on occasion the desire not to be a burden or nuisance to hard-pressed relatives. It is difficult to think of it as other than a failure in faith in God and his suffering grace. And it must also be a matter of self-searching for those who are left with feelings of guilt for not being able to have perceived the breaking point. One wonders if the moment after death is any less painful than the moment before death, when in the clearer light of eternity one's conscience would accept responsibility.

Mother Jane gives us a prayer by Victor Stock, for when we need to express in words our sadness:

A prayer for one who took her own life
O God Righteous and Compassionate
Forgive the despair of ——— for whom we pray.
Heal in her that which is broken
And in your great Love stand with those
Hurt by the violence of her end.
Lord be to her not a Judge but a Saviour:
Receive her into that Kingdom wherein by your mercy
We sinners also would have place
Through the merits of our Wounded Redeemer
Who lives and reigns with you in the Holy Spirit's
Power now and unto the Ages of Ages. Amen.
Fairacres Chronicle (Spring 1987)

Another troubling problem is the growing number of abortions, not of those who with perplexed hearts may have to decide between the life of the mother and that of the embryo, nor of the pregnancy that modern medical science is certain would result in a badly damaged life. The worrying sad problem is the growth of the idea that abortion on demand should become the norm.

The worst of these worryings could be avoided by the acceptance of contraceptive rightness, either in spacing the interval between one child and the next, or not giving birth to too many children for the health of the mother and the adequate provision and care for those already born. Birth control could also be willed conception, rather than conception being an incident or accident of even loving sexual concern. If the choice offered to people is between planned birth and abortions, there should be no doubt as to which is better for human society.

Still another worrying health hazard, peculiar to the elderly, is senile dementia, in which people of intelligence, including many brilliant people, become little more than vegetables, losing their power of memory and recognition, and sometimes liable to violent outbreaks against caring relatives. The assurance of the later Isaiah is that 'They that wait upon the Lord shall renew their strength, they shall mount up like eagles, they shall walk and not faint' (Isa. 40:31). Mark in his gospel records the teaching of Jesus about the diseases that infect and weaken the whole life, finally killing the spirit:

> Can't you see that anything that goes into a man from outside cannot make him 'common' or unclean? You see, it doesn't go into his heart, but into his stomach, and passes out of the body altogether, so that all food is clean enough. 'But,' he went on, 'whatever comes out of a man, that is what makes a man "common" or unclean. For it is from inside, from men's hearts and minds, that evil thoughts arise – lust, theft, murder, adultery, greed, wickedness, deceit, sensuality, envy, slander, arrogance and folly! All these evil things come from inside a man and make him unclean!' (Mark 7:21–23)
>
> from J. B. Phillips, *The Gospels in Modern English*

There is one radical way in which the health of 60 per cent of the world's sickness could be cured and avoided. The Stockholm Institute of Peace Studies estimates that 3000 million people in the world do not get pure drinking water.

As a result diseases of the stomach, digestion and liver develop, the most striking being dysentery, cholera, enteritis, worms infection in children; acid rain through uncontrolled emission of fumes from factories is blown by the wind from one country to another, rivers and coastal water are polluted by the sewerage that is poured into them and the impurities from manufacturing processes. We can thank God that water authorities have become aware of the dangers, and given sufficient finance could organise the catchment, storage, and filtration and supply to millions of homes. A great campaign is needed, governments to be lobbied, generous benefactors and trusts approached to make annual grants for a period of years, and millions of small subscribers enlisted to support the special projects and agencies.

Some helpful prayers:

Moods
O my Lord, when moods
of depression, anxiety, or resentment
take possession of me,
let me ask, 'Why art thou so heavy, O my soul,
and why art thou so disquieted within me?'
And let the answer show me
the cause of my mood and dispel it,
so that I forget my hurts and want only Thee.

G.A.

Diseases at present incurable
O Heavenly Father,
we pray thee for those suffering
from diseases at present incurable.
Give them the victory of trust and hope,
that they may never lose their faith
in thy loving purpose.
Grant thy wisdom to all who are working
to discover the secrets of disease,

and the faith that through Thee
all things are possible.
We ask this in the Name of him
who went about doing good
and healing all kinds of disease,
even thy Son Jesus Christ our Lord.

G.A.

For the sick in mind
O Holy Spirit who dost delve into all things,
even the deep things of God
and the deep things of man,
we pray thee to penetrate the springs of personality
of all who are sick in mind,
to bring them cleansing, healing, and unity.
Sanctify all memory, dispel all fear,
bring them to love Thee
with all their mind and will,
that they may be made whole
and glorify Thee for ever.
We ask this in the Name of him
who cast out devils and healed men's minds,
even Jesus Christ our Lord.

G.A.

Renewal
O my God,
grant that I may so wait upon Thee,
that when quick decision and action are needed
I may mount up with wings as an eagle;
and when under direction of thy will
and the needs of people
I have to keep going under pressure,
I may run and not be weary;
and in times of routine and humble duty,
I may walk and not faint.

For all my fresh springs are in Thee,
O God of my strength.

G.A.

all from *One Man's Prayers*

20

Praying about World Issues

4500 million people in the world, so many that the mind boggles and official records find it easier to identify us by numbers, often of nine figures, rather than by name. Individuals wonder about their own personal value and people who pray doubt whether their prayers can have any effect on the difficult situations facing humanity today.

Natural catastrophes – earthquakes, volcanic eruptions, hurricanes, floods – take place; weapons are more deadly than ever and seemingly easy to produce; the technically advanced nations engage in arms trade, developing nations make the purchase of arms a priority, explosions are set off by remote control; food surpluses are piled up, unscrupulous people corner markets and send up prices. Anyone who reads the daily papers or who scans the headlines, or listens to a brief summary of the daily news, can lengthen the list of tragedies – crimes, cruelties and heartbreaks. What can one individual do, or a church congregation or a political party? Things often seem to have got out of hand, God's hand as well as ours!

Jesus in his great prayer taught his followers to pray that God's good name should be guarded, that his will should be done and be seen to be done, that he should be allowed to rule in our hearts and affairs. These great prayers were ones that he put into practice as well as prayed. If we count ourselves as his disciples, we too must pray for the world and for God.

The first answer to our questioning is that our prayer keeps such situations tied to God and prevents him being forgotten or pushed out. Our faith in him, confirmed in our personal contact with him in experience, is that he is present even in the worst situations. Many Jews went into the gas chambers undaunted, believing that God went with them, and God being spirit and the human spirit created by him, cannot be incinerated.

A second clue comes from St Paul, who taught us that man-made situations arise from wrong attitudes within our minds and spirits, so that our struggle is a spiritual one, and not against human enemies. The prophet Elisha when shut up in the little town of Dothan by invading troops could see that there was a much greater army of spiritual troops, so that he could say to his trembling young attendant, 'They that be with us are more than they that be with them.' Centuries later Paul was able to say that if God is for us, who can ultimately stand against us. What we have to make sure is that we are on God's side, in trust and rightness.

The psychologist Jung believed that there is a common unconscious in which we are all included and so can influence the psychic dimension. Each one of us is like a little knot in the network of human relations, in which little impulses of goodness can be transmitted, and through which the infinitely greater energy of God can flow.

Thy Kingdom come! on bended knee
    the passing ages pray;
and faithful souls have yearned to see
    on earth that Kingdom's day;

The day in whose clear-shining light
    all wrong shall stand revealed,
when justice shall be throned in might
    and every heart be healed;

When knowledge, hand in hand with peace,

shall walk the earth abroad,
the day of perfect righteousness,
the promised day of God.

F. L. Hosmer (1840–1929)
from *Hymns A. & M.* (rev.) 263

The kingdom of the world has become the kingdom of
our Lord and of his Christ, and he will reign for ever and
ever. (Rev. 11:15)

21

Praying for World Peace

St Paul, writing to the small group of Christians in Philippi, for whom he had a special affection, urged them, 'Have no anxiety about anything, but in everything by prayer and supplication with thanksgiving let your requests be made known to God' (Phil. 4:6). That would seem to be a text well worth deep study for all who feel a special call to pray for peace.

So following Paul's advice, we offer our anxieties, our hopes and prayers to God with thanksgiving. Indeed there is much to be thankful for. I thank God for the revelation of himself, his will and purpose, his universal love, his unlimited forgiveness, his eternal purpose to gather the whole human race into the divine love (John 11:51–52). We should praise him for the assurance that is given us in the Bible that he is always at work even in the worst of circumstances to redeem the most dismaying happenings. We can be grateful for the stirring of conscience everywhere about the tragedy and waste of war, and for the many conferences and demonstrations that are taking place, aimed at avoiding war and finding the way to peace. We can thank God for the growth of compassion among the nations shown through the immediate aid in emergency and disaster situations, and through pattern activities like Christian Aid, Catholic Action, Oxfam, Save the Children Fund, War on Want and others.

I do not hesitate to thank God that governments, nations

and political parties are sensitive to public opinion, moral pressure and informed protest, especially when a general election is near. I thank him too that the religions of the world are beginning to think and work together for human welfare, social justice and world peace, though much more needs to be done in pursuing those three fundamental aims. Few people know that there is now a Conference of Religions for World Peace (CRWP) which has already held four world assemblies. More and more people are taking part in the annual Week of Prayer for World Peace, which has until recently published its material for prayer in English, but is now planning to publish it in the main languages of the world, so that people of all faiths may join together to pray in their own way and in their own language.

In that hope we go on to pray for the tasks that still have to be done. First and foremost we must pray for the scaling down of fear in the hearts of all people. Mahatma Gandhi urged us, 'Do not fear, he who fears hates; he who hates kills. Break your sword and throw it away, and fear will not touch you. I have been delivered from desire and from fear, so that I know the power of God.'

Archbishop Michael Ramsey has given us this insight: 'The human race is afraid and its fears are about power – about having it or not having it. Those who have it are frightened that they may be going to lose it. Those who do not have it are frightened of those with it. This is true of groups, classes, nations and races.' Often we may feel powerless to do anything effective for the cause of peace. At such times we may pray:

O God whose blessed Son was powerless in the hands of men and was content to be nailed to be the cross when those who had brought him there jeered at his inability to save himself, yet did not fail in love towards all who had a hand in his death: Grant that when we have no power, we may exercise the power of love, and pray that thy righteous and loving will be done, as it was by thy blessed Son, revealing thy unfailing love and unlimited forgiveness.

G.A.

We must be aware that there are many situations in the world today in which people do well to be afraid. Father Timothy Rees (died 1939) wrote an accusing hymn after the First World War which is as pertinent today as it was then. Two verses particularly move me to pray:

Christ crucified today
Wherever love is outraged,
   wherever hope is killed,
Where man still wrongs his brother man,
   thy Passion is fulfilled.
We see thy tortured body,
   we see the wounds that bleed,
Where brotherhood hangs crucified,
   nailed to the cross of greed.

The groaning of creation,
   wrung out by pain and care,
The anguish of a million hearts
   that break in dumb despair;
O crucified Redeemer,
   these are thy cries of pain;
O may they break our selfish hearts,
   and love come in to reign.

Timothy Rees (1874–1939)
from *100 Hymns for Today*

I need not elaborate, for the daily newspapers chronicle the endemic cruelty and anguish.

Let me continue in the thanksgiving which can accompany even our most anguished prayers. I thank God for Pope

John Paul II for calling together the leaders of the world religions to pray with him for peace, and for his prayers at Hiroshima in the name of the multitudes in every country and in every period of history 'who do not want war and are ready to walk the road to peace'. We can thank God for Cardinal Basil Hume's tenderness of heart for all suffering children and the thousands who die prematurely every day. We are grateful for Bob Geldoff, pleading so effectively for himself and for the younger generation. We can thank God for Bruce Kent who has made nuclear disarmament take priority of his priesthood, and for Gordon Wilson of the Anglican Pacifist Fellowship, so well-informed about what is going on in the world, so wise in his advice to workers for peace.

The Venerable Htich Hnat Hanh is the head of the Buddhist Peace Mission and has his headquarters in Paris. His plea that 'man is not our enemy' reminds me of St Paul's words to the Ephesians when speaking of the whole armour of God: 'For we are not contending against flesh and blood, but against principalities, against the powers, against the world rulers of this present darkness, against the spiritual hosts of wickedness in the heavenly places' (6:12). The enemies we have to fight are hatred, jealousy, greed, untruths, mistaken ideas of God, 'envy, hatred, malice and all uncharitableness', as the 1662 litany puts it.

The weapons which go to make up the whole armour of God are the belt of truth, the breastplate of righteousness, the shield of faith, shoes quick to take the message of peace, the helmet of trust in God's protecting love, the sword of the spirit which is the word of God, piercing through all confusions and pretences (Eph. 6:13–20). Those are the only weapons we Christians are permitted to use.

People often wonder how our prayers for peace and other great world issues can affect such situations. Tragic things happen, cruel deeds are done, things seem to have got out of hand, God's hand as well as ours. How can the prayers

of individuals or even congregations help to cure such tragedies and widespread evil? The first answer I have mentioned
before, that our prayers keep such situations tied to God
and prevent him being pushed out.

The second clue is that most man-made situations arise
from wrong attitudes within the minds and spirits of people,
so that the struggle is basically a spiritual one. Prayer is a
spiritual activity and operates within the spirit of the one
who prays, and also within the spirits of those prayed for.

We live today in a society in which violence is rife. The
Christian will remember the rebuke of Jesus to Peter when
he attempted a one-man rescue in the Garden of Gethsemane, and began to strike out right and left with his sword:
'Put your sword back into its place; for all who take the
sword will perish by the sword' (Matt. 26:52). This short
text tells us a great deal about 'the law of violence': it is
continuous, once you start you cannot get away from it; it
is reciprocal, others tend to do to you what you do to them;
violence is unlimited, it is not possible to say 'so far and no
further', violence simply begets violence, so the good end is
defeated by the wrong means. It is also interesting to note
that those who use violence always try to justify it.

So we must try to understand the causes of violence and
the bitterness of people who feel that a great injustice has
been inflicted on them. At the same time we must try to
introduce into situations of tension and violence something
specifically spiritual. When I was Anglican Archbishop in
Jerusalem two Arab priests told me they were members of
the Palestinian Liberation Organisation (PLO). I felt that I
had no right to object to their political association, but I
did feel it right to remind them that they were Christ's
representatives within the PLO and that they should pray
and work for a just and agreed solution.

It is good for Christians to know that there are people in
other religious traditions who care as passionately as we
profess to do, about suffering and reconciliation. For

example, the Buddhist Vietnamese monk Htich Hnat Hanh, at the height of the Vietnam war, wrote this poem of anguished appeal:

Promise me, promise me, this day
while the sun is at its zenith
even as they strike you down
with a mountain of hate and violence,
remember, brother, man is not our enemy.
Alone again, I'll go on
with bent head, but knowing
the immortality of love.

Professor Hasan Askari, a very ecumenical Muslim and a devoted practitioner of meditation, prays: 'O God, You are the King; You are the All Holy; You are the All-Peace; Guide us into Your Kingdom, into the paths of Peace.'

There is a more wholesome kind of fear common to both parties when war is threatened or actually breaks out, namely the realisation of the immense destructive power in nuclear energy. In the first atomic bomb dropped on Hiroshima 60,000 people were killed in a blinding, burning flash, and a similar number died from the effects of radiation. Nuclear bombs today are infinitely more powerful. Realistic fear of retaliation has kept rival nations from nuclear war for over forty years, and for that fact we must be thankful, even though it is said that Russia has enough nuclear weapons to kill everyone in the USA ten times over, and similarly the USA has enough nuclear weapons to do the same to the people of Russia. Our litany for peace must include some such petition as, 'From all overkill, save us and help us we humbly beseech Thee, O Lord', and then go on to pray for raising the world's valuation of human life to God's level, thanking him for his love and care for every single human being and for his plan that mankind shall live together as his family, in the kind of world that he has always been working to create.

To be dedicated workers for peace we need to have peace in our own hearts. So we may pray:

> O God of many names
> Lover of all nations
> We pray for peace
>   in our hearts
>   in our homes
>   in our nation
>   in our world
> the peace of your will
> the peace of our need.

G.A.

Each of us can pray in our own words, repeating some short sentences: 'Guide our feet into the way of peace' or 'Give peace in our time, O God' or just saying the word Peace, Pax, Shalom, Salaam, Shanti, and adding to the word in our own language the appeal to the God of peace, through the Prince of peace.

At other times I have practised a devotional meditation which is an extension of a 'prayer' or aspiration of the Buddha: 'Now may every living thing, young or old, weak or strong, living near or far, known or unknown, living or departed or yet unborn, may every living thing be full of bliss.'

One can sit with a quiet heart and mind and send out a radiation of love, joy, compassion and peace in turn, beginning with one's home, neighbourhood, country, other countries, the whole world, and then to those in the spiritual sphere whom we speak of as 'dead', but could more truthfully be described as 'risen ones'.

Let me close with what is to me the decisive imperative in the thinking, practice and praying of all who profess to be Christian peacemakers. It comes from St Paul's second letter to the disciples at Corinth, and it needs no para-phrasing or embellishment:

If anyone is in Christ, he is a new creation; the old has passed away, behold, the new has come. All this is from God, who through Christ reconciled us to himself and gave us the ministry of reconciliation; that is, in Christ God was reconciling the world to himself, not counting their trespasses against them, and entrusting to us the message of reconciliation. So we are ambassadors for Christ, God making his appeal through us. (2 Cor. 5:17-20).

Further prayers which may be prayed on appropriate occasions:

The long travail of mankind
Grant us to look with your eyes of compassion,
O merciful God, at the long travail of mankind:
the wars, the hungry millions,
the countless refugees,
the natural disasters,
the cruel and needless deaths,
men's inhumanity to one another,
the heartbreak and hopelessness of so many lives.
Hasten the coming of the messianic age
when the nations shall be at peace,
and men shall live free from fear
and free from want
and there shall be no more pain or tears,
in the security of your will,
the assurance of your love,
the coming of your Kingdom,
O God of Righteousness, O Lord of Compassion.

G.A.
from *Jerusalem Prayers*

The ways to peace
Lord God of Righteousness, we know that Your will is
peace on earth and that You call all your children to pray
and work for peace. Holy Father, we differ in our hopes
how peace may come: some believe in a deterrent and
pray that it may truly deter; others pray that peace may
come through seemingly safer means. Lord God, look not,
we pray You on our divisions, but on our united fear that
nuclear war will exterminate the life that You have given.
Inspire and strengthen us in the ministry of reconciliation
laid upon us by your beloved Son our beloved Lord, Jesus
Christ.

G.A.

O God, the heart fails in the thought of the millions who
die before they find the full enjoyment of life as you
intend it to be – deaths through war, hunger, violence and
disease. We know that you are the giver and sustainer of
life, extending it beyond man's short span, into the spiritual and eternal. O God, I dare to ask for eternal life for
every soul, now and beyond death: I pray this prayer
through my touch with Jesus Christ, eternal Son and
eternal brother.

G.A.
from *In His Name*

For the right use of power
Almighty and merciful God, without whom all things
hasten to destruction and fall into nothingness: Look, we
beseech Thee, upon thy family of nations and men, to
which thou hast committed power in trust for their mutual
health and comfort. Save us and help us, O Lord, lest we
abuse thy gift and make it our misery and ruin; draw all
men unto thee in thy kingdom of righteousness and truth;
uproot our enmities, heal our divisions, cast out our fears;
and renew our faith in thine unchanging purpose of

goodwill and peace on earth; for the love of Jesus Christ
our Lord.

F. B. MacNutt
The Prayer Manual

Divine discontent
Hasten the time, O Lord, when no man shall live in
contentment while he knows that others have need.
Inspire in us and in people of all nations the desire for
social justice, that the hungry may be fed, the homeless
welcomed, the sick healed, and a just order established in
the world, according to thy gracious will made known in
Jesus Christ, our Lord.

G.A.
from *One Man's Prayers*

A great happening
O God, we thank Thee that the nations are learning the
compassion of our Lord, Jesus Christ. Grant that our
nation may give generously for the relief of the homeless
and that our people may welcome the refugee. Help us in
our plenty to remember the needs of others and never to
grudge the cost of helping them; for his sake who did not
grudge the cross, but gave himself for all, even Jesus
Christ, our Lord.

G.A.
(ibid.)

O Heavenly Father, we thank thee for those who out of
the bitter memories of strife and loss are seeking a more
excellent way for the nations of the world, whereby justice
and order may be maintained and the differences of
peoples be resolved in equity. We pray thee to establish
their purpose on sure foundations and to prosper their

labours, that thy will may be seen to be done; as shown us in the human life of Jesus Christ our Lord.

Unknown
from *In His Name*

Prayed at Assisi, October 1986
We pray that we and all men and women may firmly exclude violence as a solution to personal, community and world problems, that leaders and governments may refuse to be involved in the arms race, that every human person may reject everything that could lead to nuclear conflict, offering instead human understanding, tolerance, mutual respect and reconciliation.

Human rights (at Assisi)
We pray that we and all our fellow human beings may grow in respect for human dignity and its inalienable rights; may we use our liberty with scrupulous care not to infringe the rights of others, having a practical concern for their needs and facing conflicts with mutual respect, understanding (and unfailing hope).

22

Invaded or Invading

In much younger years I used to think of the Christian as an individual and the Church as always being on the defence against the attacks of evil. I see now that this deduction of mine and of many other Christians was based on a conversation which Jesus had with his disciples about what people were saying about him. He followed it up with a more personal and pointed question, 'What do you say about me?' Peter in a flash of conviction was the first to answer: 'You are the Christ, the Son of the Living God'.

Jesus, grateful for this recognition, assured him that it was on the rock of this faith that he would build his Church, and promised that the gates of hell should not prevail against it. My incomplete interpretation was that the focus of evil and the powers of death should not prevail against a Church built on such a foundation. That was true enough as far as it went, but the assumption in my mind was that the Church would be able to defend itself against such attack. It took some years before I realised that the Church was not meant to be a beleaguered city but an invading force of goodness and love. The gates of hell, Jesus asserted, would not be able to repel the army of God.

A Jewish poet speaks of the hardship of those who were returning from exile and says of God 'He has broken the gates of brass, and smitten the bars of iron in sunder' (Ps. 107:16). Prisoners held captive will be released into freedom and full life.

John in exile on Patmos in deep meditation sees the forces of evil being driven out of heaven. Evil personified in the devil is banished from the presence of God. He still operates on earth, but we are warned and heartened that his time is short and therefore his resistance will be fierce.

Evil is not eternal, it does not exist in its own right. It is only the negation of good. Julian, the anchoress of Norwich in the fourteenth century, in the showings she received about the being and nature of God, perceived this non-eternal nature of evil which she put in the words 'Evil is no thing'. The forces of evil recognised in Jesus a threat to their own power. So they brought against him not only the temptation that comes to all humans, but disguised devilish suggestions, subtle distortions of good, deflections of the divine will. Their final resort was to kill him, but the very act of accepting this killing only showed the invincibility of love, the limitlessness of divine forgiveness, the perfection of trust in God. The resurrection was God's seal on the life, death and survival in the face of all that devils and men could inflict on him.

So we in our century need to be alerted to evil, to recognise it in ourselves and in our human societies, but we can be heartened by our Lord's words, 'Be of good cheer, I have overcome the world'. As Baring Gould's triumphant hymn asserts, 'Gates of hell can never 'gainst that Church prevail, We have Christ's own promise, and that cannot fail.' The gates of hell are open wide, prison doors stand open, every curtain on the way to God is torn from top to bottom.

Possible prayers:

Thou art risen, O Lord!
Let the gospel trumpets speak,
   and the news as of holy fire,
    burning and flaming and inextinguishable,
    run to the ends of the earth.

Thou art risen, O Lord!
Let all creation greet the good tidings
    with jubilant shout;
  for its redemption has come,
  the long night is past, the Saviour lives!
  and rides and reigns in triumph
    now and unto the ages of ages.

Eric Milner-White
from *In His Name*

Bring me my bow of burning gold!
  Bring me my arrows of desire!
Bring me my spear! O clouds, unfold!
  Bring me my chariot of fire!
I will not cease from mental fight,
  Nor shall my sword sleep in my hand,
Till we have built Jerusalem
  In England's green and pleasant land.

William Blake

Rank on rank the host of heaven spreads its
    vanguard on the way,
As the Light of light descendeth from the
    realms of endless day,
That the powers of hell may vanish as the darkness
    clears away.

Liturgy of St James
(tr. G. Moultrie) from *English Hymnal* 318

23

Holy Mother Church?

Immediately after the spiritual experience of his baptism when he felt God's approval of his intention and action and the inflow of grace and power, Jesus obeyed an irresistible urge to go apart into the desert countryside around Jericho, to discover from the Father how he should exercise his vocation as God's Son and Messiah.

Forty days later he began to recruit a band of disciples whom he could train to be partners in his mission. That step was the first result of his forty days Moses-like retreat. He began with men who had been inspired by the fiery preaching of his cousin John and his symbolic practice of washing and drowning and a fresh start. Another inspiration was to seek for twelve men, one for every tribe of the nation, who believed they were a people loved and chosen by God, who needed to learn that they had no monoply of God. So the twelve were called – Andrew, John, Andrew's brother Peter, John's brother James, Philip living among a colony of Greeks, Nathaniel the guileless one – the whole list can be seen in Matthew 10:2-4, followed by guidelines for the mission to the towns and villages of Galilee, preparing the way for his own visitation.

A more comprehensive charter of blessings, interpretations and duties of the new order can be seen in Matthew 5-7, which need careful and prayerful study of how to adapt that manifesto for today.

Gradually that original local mission began to be seen as

the embryo of world mission, expressed clearly in a final
command in the climax of Matthew's memoirs. They were
told to go to all nations, with his authority, to preach, to
teach, to baptise, added to his earlier instructions: to heal
in spirit, mind and body, with the glorious assurance that he
whom critics and opponents thought they were liquidating
by killing him, would be with them in his risen and deathless
life (Matt. 28:19–20).

The writer of the fourth gospel, the disciple whom Jesus
loved and who understood Jesus most deeply, confirms this
interpretation of world mission in the last prayer with the
first twelve missioners before they set off to Gethsemane.
No biblical scholars or meditating disciple can surpass the
spirit and love of that prayer in John 17, when Jesus prays
not only for the twelve, but for all down the ages who should
come to believe in his revelation of the sacred heart of God
and his own gratitude and love for the twelve men – and for
the devoted women disciples who came to the sepulchre
while it was still dark and heard a divine word within their
grieving hearts, 'He is not here . . . He is risen. Why do you
seek the living among the dead?' An hour later the risen
One urges Mary Magdalene not to hold him earthbound,
for he is with the Father, his Father and the universal Father,
transcendent yet immanent, abolishing the great gulf which
people thought of as separating God from man, the living
now from the still living who have made the great migration
with him.

The great apostle, the much-loved and very-loving disciple
John, fifty or more years later, in lonely banishment on
Patmos, has the continuing experience of the ubiquity and
eternity of the crucified and risen Christ: 'Fear not, I am the
first and the last, I died, and behold I am alive for evermore
. . . and I have the keys of death and Hades' the after-world,
the under-world and the eternal world '. . . write what you
see and send it to the churches.'

So the Church is founded on the love of the cross and the

glory of the resurrection, and is to be Christ's spiritual body, through which he will carry on his saving love until the end of the world, until the end of time, which may be millions of years ahead. The unnamed writer of the Epistle to the Hebrews has another symbolic figure which helps us to image the pioneer and perfecter of our faith:

> Since then we have a great high priest who has passed through the heavens, Jesus, the Son of God, let us hold fast our confession. For we have not a high priest who is unable to sympathise with our weaknesses, but one who in every respect has been tempted as we are, yet without sin. Let us then with confidence draw near to the throne of grace, that we may receive mercy and find grace to help in time of need. (Heb. 4:14–16)

The prologue of St John's gospel sums up our search for words and images which can confirm our faith and help us to witness to it:

> In the beginning was the Word, and the Word was with God and the Word was God . . . In him was life and the life was the light of the world . . . The true light that enlightens every man coming into the world . . . And the Word became flesh and dwelt among us, full of grace and truth; we have beheld his glory . . . No one has ever seen God; the only Son, who is in the bosom (*heart*) of the Father he has made him known. (John 1:1–18)

Christ is called 'the Word of God', because through him God speaks and explains himself and his will to all human beings, in all generations, of every race, nation, language, speaking to the heart of everyone.

In the Nicene Creed, amplified at Constantinople in 480, we confess our faith in 'one, holy, catholic and apostolic church'. Looking at the history of the Church we cannot see those words as true of its present condition. They describe the Church as it is in the mind of God and his will, the Church as it ought to be.

Maria Boulding of Stanbrook Abbey, in her great book *The Coming of God*, says of the Christian Church:

> It is the place of embodied grace, of promise and covenant, but its history is stained by every kind of sin and betrayal. It has its epics of holiness but they are unequivocably attributed to God. Ringing in the ears of its members is the warning, 'To whom much is given, of them much is required'.

Sister Maria also speaks of the Church's responsibility for the world and implies the failure of the Church to lead the nations into the ways of peace:

> We have dire need of peace. Super-powers with weapons of unimaginable destructiveness are only the outward manifestation of threatening chaos, because the forces which destroy peace are within our own hearts, and we can wreck our civilization unaided by giving them free play. These are greed and grabbing, ruthless consumerism where there should be reverence and stewardship, the habit of preferring our own short-term advantages to the common good for which society insists, a cleverness untempered by wisdom, a spiritual blindness and ubiquitous fear. We need a peace that will heal the divisions within us and exorcise the fear which looks to violence as the only way to maintain ourselves against the threats from without.

Christians share in this chronic human condition and have the responsibility of bringing the justice, grace, reconciliation and forgiveness of God into it.

Sceptics, critics and commentators say that the Church has

failed in another way, namely that very few people are now regular churchgoers. They, like some churchgoers, think that religion is little more than attendance in church. There are however occasions when there is a good attendance, namely at baptisms, confirmations, weddings and funerals, services which are related to the span of human life, when minister, members of the family, friends, rejoice with those who do rejoice, look with hope to the future and feel for those who mourn, with warm identification and friendship.

A more blameworthy criticism of the churches is our failure to fulfil our Lord's prayer for the unity of all his disciples, that the world may believe in his coming from God. Many of us talk of things prayed for as 'coming in God's good time', as if it all depended on him rather than our response to his will and eager acceptance of his grace, forgetful of the biblical declaration that now is the accepted time. So when we pray with that great apostle of unity, the Abbé Couturier, we should perhaps underline the second part of his prayer: pray for the unity of the Church according to the will of Christ and in the way that he will show us.

The following prayers may be helpful when we need words rather than silence:

Grant, O God, that the Church may be the people of God, the embodiment of Christ, the community of love, thy Servant to all in all generations. Grant it unity, holiness, zeal and fire that it may be the agent of thy loving Will to gather the whole human race into thy divine love. We ask this in faith through Jesus Christ, the Lord of the Church, our beloved Saviour and thy beloved Son.

O Lord of the Church help us to be the Church of the Lord. We need your grace to make the Church one and heal our divisions, to make the Church holy in all her members and in all her branches, to make her truly catholic – for all people and in all truth, to make her apostolic, with the faith and zeal of your first apostles, dear Lord of the Church.

We may also pray often St Paul's great prayer for the churches around Ephesus, which we have found equally inspiring and relevant in our meditation on all human families and the need to be rooted and grounded in the divine love (Eph. 3:14–19).

A personal dedication
Thee will I love and serve
  Now in time's passing day;
Thy hand shall hold me fast
  When time is done away
In God's unknown eternal spheres
To serve Him through eternal years.

Canon G. W. Briggs

A final Gloria
Into thy hands, our Father, we commit this thy world, this thy family, for which our Lord Jesus Christ was content to be betrayed, and to suffer death upon the cross. Into thy hands we commit thy universal Church and her unity. Into thy hands we commit all the problems which seem insoluble, in sure and certain hope; for in Thee is our trust. Here and now, we lay all in thy hands. All love, all glory, be unto Thee, for ever and ever.

Olive Wyon

24

One Thing Needful

If anyone was asked what he or she wanted more than anything else, I wonder what the answer would be. For me, looking back on a long and adventurous life, I think I can say honestly that the thing that has helped me most can be summed up in a four-letter word – love.

When we were very young loving tenderness was what we subconsciously needed, and if we did not receive it things went wrong and we spent the rest of our lives looking for it. Being taken into care may have provided food, clothing, some kind of a home, some kind of education, but if there was no love, something was tragically missing.

When we are very old, however comfortable we may be, however successful we may have been, however big the bank balance may be, life seems empty if there is no love. A priest friend of mine had a very successful businessman living in his parish, with whom he became extremely friendly. One day he congratulated this successful friend, only to be told, 'Yes, I have made a fortune, but in doing so I made money the most important thing in my life, and as a result I lost the love of my wife and children.'

There are people who do not believe in God, who believe that love is the most important value in life. Bertrand Russell, a philosopher but not a believer in God, once surprised a university audience by saying that Christian love or compassion was the thing most needed by modern man. 'If you have Christian love', he declared, 'you have a motive for existence, a guide for action, a reason for courage, an imperative necessity for intellectual honesty.' We religious people must be careful lest we think we have a monopoly of human and divine love.

I have a great admiration and affection for St Paul with his great mind, his respect for the Roman empire, his awareness of being a world citizen, but from those attributes alone I would never have thought he could have written the greatest poem on love. Without love, he declared, 'my preaching is little more than clanging cymbals'. He added an analysis of love that would inspire anyone wanting to practise it:

> Love is very patient, very kind. Love knows no jealousy; love makes no parade, gives itself no airs, is never rude, never selfish, never irritated, never resentful; love is never glad when others go wrong, love is gladdened by goodness, always slow to expose, always eager to believe the best, always hopeful, always patient. Love never disappears. (1 Cor. 13:4–8, tr. Moffatt)

We have already studied Paul's prayer for his flock at Ephesus, in which he prays that they may know the four dimensions of love – length, height, depth and breadth – of which we become conscious when Christ incarnates himself in us (Eph. 3:14–19). The depth and comprehensiveness of that prayer increases every time we Christians pray it.

St John, conscious of our Lord's love for him, urges the readers of his first letter: 'Beloved, let us love one another; for love is of God, and he who loves is born of God and knows God' (4:7), adding that love is the essence of God's being, character and will: 'God is love, and he who abides in love abides in God, and God abides in him' (4.16b). He continues with the insight that we only really begin to live when we love, and those who do not love are spiritually dead (3:14).

In his gospel John gives us what is for many the key verse of the Bible: 'God so loved the world that he gave his only Son that whoever believes in him should not perish but have eternal life' (3:16). It was to prove the truth of this that Jesus went to the cross, and also to emphasise the fact of God's forgiveness. Only if we love are we truly children of God and disciples of his Son. This love must extend to the whole of humanity and must be undefeatable. Jesus said that it must even include enemies, for ultimately it is the only thing that can turn enemies into friends. It has a cosmic significance.

There are many unloving situations in the world today, many unloving people, many whom we may find difficult to love. St John of the Cross, a Spanish mystic of the sixteenth century, gives us a principle for such sad situations: 'Where there is no love, pour love in, and you will draw love out.' That is what God is always doing, and if we really believe that we are his children we shall want to do the same, in the way shown to us by his perfect Son, our elder brother.

Prayers to pray:

O Lord, who hast taught us that all our doings without charity are nothing worth; Send thy Holy Ghost, and pour into our hearts that most excellent gift of charity, the very bond of peace and of all virtues, without which whosoever liveth is counted dead before thee: Grant this for thine only Son Jesus Christ's sake.

BCP, Quinquagesima

Eternal God, whose image lies in the hearts of all
 people,
We live among peoples whose ways are different from
 ours,
 whose faiths are foreign to us,
 whose tongues are unintelligible to us.

Help us to remember that you love all people with your
    great love,
  that all religion is an attempt to respond to you,
  that the yearnings of other hearts are much like our
    own and are known to you.
Help us to recognize you in the words of truth, the things
    of beauty, the actions of love about us.
We pray through Christ, who is a stranger to no one land
    more than another, and to every land no less than to
    another.

World Council of Churches
(Vancouver Assembly 1983)

25

Christians in a Secularised World

What does it mean to be a Christian in the world today, so different from the world in which the prophets lived and warned; and different also to the world in which Jesus for three short years made it his priority to reveal the universal and eternal Father and the perfect rightness, wisdom and love of the Father's will, being willing to live and to die to show that double truth in terms of a human life and an excruciatingly painful death. His hope and faith was that by being lifted in love on a cross of shame and pain, he would draw all humans to himself and through him to the God of forgiveness and love.

Studying the sacred scriptures and records of the ancient and modern world it would seem that true believers and people of holy character have always been a minority, and that is so today. Many people, speaking more truly than they know, describe themselves as nominal Christians or use that term in critical judgment of others.

Statistics are quoted to show the decline in churchgoing, and a fall in the number of baptisms, confirmations, marriages in church, vocations to the ministry. It is however in Sunday observance that most people measure the decline, expressed in a demand for shops to be opened, great sporting fixtures arranged, which necessitate transport facilities, involving people who would rather not work on Sundays except in most cases for the attraction of overtime rates of pay.

Humanity owes a great debt of gratitude to the Jews who, under the leadership of Moses the lawgiver, accepted the principle of one day in seven for rest, recreation and worship. Moses, having led the Israelites safely out of Egypt, called a halt at Mt Sinai, while he went up into the mountain for forty days to find out from the mind of God the laws by which the liberated people should live. The fourth of the basic commandments was that the seventh day should be a day of rest when none but emergency work should be done, that day being a Sabbath of the Lord. The book of Leviticus contains the laws of worship, and also the second great commandment, to love one's neighbour as oneself (19:18), the first being to love God with all one's heart and mind and will (Deut. 6:4–9). Before they moved on from Sinai the nation made a solemn covenant to keep God's commandments, in return for which they believed that they would be a chosen people, guided and blessed by God.

The Sabbath rest from work was to be enjoyed by slaves and by foreigners as well as by the whole family. St Luke's gospel tells us that it was the custom of Jesus to attend the synagogue on the Sabbath day (4:16). In time his followers changed the day to the first day of the week, combining with it the thankful remembrance of his resurrection. Muslims too have a weekly holy day, and the Friday mosque with its prostrations in worship is well attended. All three theistic communities would be reluctant to change their sacred day, but in the West it is Christians who are most concerned about a completely secular and commercial Sunday. Should the legal requirements be changed, we Christians would need to consider how best to preserve our pattern and time of worship, perhaps having very early morning services and much later evening worship. In our democratic age the majority makes the decisions, after paying due regard to the rights and desires of the minority. So the Christian minority ought not to expect to impose its will on the whole community, though we can explain persuasively the benefit to the lives of all and nourish the spiritual component in human personality which outlives the body.

The chapel at Heathrow and other airports may suggest an example, which would apply to every day of the week, to which people might go for a quiet quarter of an hour for reflection and remembrance of God's presence everywhere. The local churches might bear the cost of furnishing a restful and beautiful retreat in other crowded places away from the bustle outside.

Implicit in all this concern about the secularised society is the realisation that we set aside one special day to remind us that the presence of God is everywhere.

In the early years of the seventeenth century a saintly priest and poet was appointed rector of Bemerton near Salisbury. George Herbert was a priest of gentle disposition, a lover of Christian virtues and a devoted pastor to the villagers of Bemerton and Fugglestone. He died of tuberculosis in 1633 at the age of forty. A verse of one of his best-known hymns is very relevant to our present secularisation:

Seven whole days, not one in seven
  I will praise Thee;
In my heart though not in heaven
  I can raise Thee.
Small it is in this poor sort
  To enrol Thee;
E'en eternity's too short
  To extol Thee.

To live in the spirit of this verse would be a witness in our present age to both spirituality and eternity.

We may also pray for all each Sunday:

O God, whose will it is
that men should rest from their labours
and find refreshment of body, mind, and spirit:

We thank thee for our yearly holidays
and for our weekly day of rest.
Bless all those now on holiday,
help them to enjoy more fully
the beauty of countryside and sea
and the message of historic places.
Give them happy fellowship
and wholesome jollity,
and grant that they may not forget Thee,
the Creator of the natural world
and the Father of all that live,
ever working thy purposes of love,
through Jesus Christ, thy Son, our Lord.

G.A.

The poet C. Day Lewis, in 'Offertorium', a liturgy for the
secular, includes two verses which may help us in times of
faltering faith and temptations to be merely nominal
Christians:

O God in whom we half believe,
Or not believe,
Or pray like importunate children
Tugging a sleeve:
Whether man's need created you,
Or his creation seed from you,
Our creeds have overshadowed you
With terror, pain and grief . . .
If you exist, if heed our cares,
If these our offerings and prayers
Could save, if earth's entreating heirs
Are to be born to live –

Spirit in whom we half believe
And would believe,
Free us from fear, revive us in
A fire of love.

from *Requiem of the Living*

Finally for clergy and people in their guardian care for our cathedrals, churches and chapels, the prayer at the entrance of the Pleshey Retreat House, which owes much to Evelyn Underhill:

Father, we pray Thee to fill this house with thy Spirit:

Here may the strong renew their strength and seek for their waking hours a noble consecration:

Here may the poor find succour and the friendless friendship:

Here may the tempted find power, the sorrowing comfort, and the bereaved find the truth that death hath no dominion over their beloved:

Here let the fearing find a new courage and the doubting have their faith and hope confirmed:

Here may the careless be awakened and all that are oppressed be freed:

Hither may many be drawn by thy love and go hence, their doubts resolved and faith renewed, their fears at rest, their courage high, their purpose firm, their sins forgiven, and their hearts aflame with thy love:

through Jesus Christ our Lord.

A hymn of faith
All praise to thee, Eternal Lord,
Who on the primal chaos of the world didst brood
And looking aeons ahead in love's creative mood
     A universe didst see.
     Creator Lord, continue thy eternal plan.

     The cell of life to matter's stuff
Was knit, and clothed the rock with herb and tree
As though preparing food for creatures yet to be,
     Pastures for flock and herd.
     Creator Lord, continue thy eternal plan.

     Then in the waters life did stir
And in the slow unhurried passing of the years
Complexity, succeeding simpler forms, appears.
     Creatures of air and land
Set forward, Lord, another stage of thy eternal plan.

Upward and onward moving then,
The spreading tree of life fresh branches grew,
Some stayed content, decling progress new,
     Good in each kind complete
     Yet not good enough for thy eternal plan.

     The main stem still continued straight
Developing new form and brain and hand until,
As aeons passed, on earth a creature thou didst fill
     With spirit kin to thine,
And galaxies with angels hymned the birth of man.

     Unfinished yet, this child of thine
Had yet to learn the secrets of his world and hour.
Seed life and harvest, fire, and atom's endless power
     Subdue and guide and use;
No limit, Lord, to thy eternal plan.

     The universe awaits the finished man,
The tree of life has still its final height to climb,

Unending years demand some focal point of time:
    This thou hast given, O Lord,
  In one short life, thyself hast said, 'Behold the man'.

  In him was life, the animating force,
Evolver of the universe, the power that moves the whole,
The light that lightens every man, in mind and heart and
    soul,
    Unrecognized before, yet speaking now,
  The Word that manifests the love in thy great plan.

  Can purpose ever cease? Ahead
Must lie new worlds of wonder, higher, fuller life,
A unity of God-like love, defeated death,
    So man with God shall look
  At their joint workmanship, and both declare it good.

  The eye of faith still peers ahead
Through human fog and dawn's receding gloom,
The final scene, no catastrophic fiery doom,
    But God's perfected plan
  When Christ shall offer back the universe and Man.

                          G.A.
                 from *One Man's Prayers*